PROGRAMMING CONCEPTS IN PYTHON

PROGRAMMING CONCEPTS IN PYTHON

ROBERT BURNS

Library of Congress Control Number: 2015908930
ISBN: Hardcover 978-1-5035-7555-4
Softcover 978-1-5035-7557-8
eBook 978-1-5035-7556-1

Print information available on the last page.

Rev. date: 06/16/2015

To order additional copies of this book, contact:
Xlibris
1-888-795-4274
www.Xlibris.com
Orders@Xlibris.com
703563

Introduction

Computers are great! You give them "input" and they produce "output". Whether it's typing an Internet address and then seeing a web page with the latest news, or entering tax information and then printing a 1040 form with all supporting documents, or using an app on a smart phone to pay for your coffee, computers offer various ways for us to specify input and they have a variety of different ways to express their output.

Computers are fast and accurate. Humans, by comparison are slow and, let's face it, we make mistakes. Have you ever added the same list of numbers twice and gotten two different totals? But humans have something that computers do not – *intelligence*.

Computers did not design the Internet, nor did they devise the tax code. Computers did not design how smart phone touch screens work. It's the humans who figured out all of that. Somewhere along the line, a human must have *explained* to a computer just exactly what to do with the input in order to turn it into output. A human had to tell the computer how to decide if a password is valid or not. A human had to explain how to calculate amortization. A human had to define the "pinch" motion and decide how it should zoom out on a photo. Same for the "shake" motion that shuffles songs in an MP3 player.

So it's the *human+computer team* that makes all of this work. Using their intelligence, the humans have the ideas and figure out "recipes" for converting input into output. Using their speed and accuracy, the computers faithfully and reliably perform the conversions.

The humans on such teams are called "programmers". The purpose of this book is to turn *you* into a programmer.

About This Book

This book is organized into three "parts", separated by major milestones in gaining programming knowledge.

Part 1 shows how to apply basic concepts of programming. It goes through the details of using freely available software to "edit" and "execute" Python programs. It shows how to store data in "variables" for use in calculations, and how to produce nice-looking output. These chapters teach all that is needed to create simple interactive programs that gather "input", perform calculations based on the input, and display "output" using calculated results.

Part 2 adds elements of logic to the simple programs of part 1. Ways are presented for making programs selectively use different sets of instructions, based on circumstances. Ways to get a program to repeat itself are also presented, allowing things to be done more than once without duplicating the steps. These chapters teach what is needed to create more sophisticated programs with "branching" and "looping" logic, such as would be required for computer games and almost every other useful program.

Part 3 introduces the powerful concept of single variables that can store multiple values all at the same time. "Array" variables can store multiple values of the same type, and are suitable for dealing with lists, such as lists of test scores, high temperatures, or names of students. "Object" variables can store multiple values of related information, and are suitable for dealing with data records, such as student accounts with names, IDs, and addresses. Chapters 13-15 introduce advanced applications of arrays and objects, for the purpose of first exposure to some advanced computer science concepts, but primarily to provide an opportunity to apply the language elements learned in parts 1 and 2.

The **Appendix** contains excerpts from the Python's built-in "functions" with references to all of the functions used in this book. There is also an **Index** at the end.

Unique Features Of This Book

Unlike many of today's introductory textbooks, this book does *not* jump into **object-oriented programming** right away. Actually, *everything* in Python is an object so you cannot really program in Python without objects. But in the sense that object-oriented *programming* means that programmers create their own "classes" that encapsulate data *and code* – that's specifically avoided. Instead, the focus is on the fundamental concepts of data, statements, expressions, and flow of control. These need to be well-understood in order to be used in the programming of classes anyway, so rather than make the student pick up both concepts at once, full treatment of objects is left for another, later level of study.

Emphasis is on **command-line execution** instead of IDEs, because it is a lowest common denominator of programming. In this way, Python program development is consistent among different systems such as PCs, Macs, and UNIX/Linux. But just about any IDE can be used in following this book, if that is the instructor's or student's choice. But because an IDE usually combines the editing and compiling steps into a single program, it's likely that the unique separation of these programming steps will be lost on the beginning student. Command-line execution makes the student more aware of the files and folders used on the host system, and differences among operating systems become not so great.

This book makes a distinction between **expressions** and **statements**. Expressions are the building blocks of statements, and as such, they individually and separately resolve to simple values that get substituted in full statements. They are likened to "phrases" in the spoken language. Language elements that are expressions are specifically pointed out as such, and are specially notated – for example, `x + y`. Full statements are likened to "sentences" in the spoken language. They are notated like this: `x = 1`. Note that these look the same as each other in the e-book format, but it's easy enough to tell the difference by context.

It may be surprising to see **linked lists, collections, and recursion** addressed in the later chapters. But the purpose is *not* to make the student proficient in the use or understanding of these concepts. Rather it is to provide a vehicle for practicing what was learned about variables, branching, loops, functions, arrays, and objects. And in so doing, the student is also introduced to ideas that will reappear in future studies in computer science, and be better prepared to learn them at that time.

This book is available in both **e-book and printed formats**, and supported by online publication of coding examples, sample assignments, and instructional how-to videos. URLs and links appear at the ends of chapters 1-14, where one might normally expect to find review questions and exercises. Go to www.rdb3.com/python/ebook for tips on navigating the e-book.

The language of the book is **common English** so as to keep it as approachable for students as possible. That's why you'll see contractions and exclamation marks!

Unique Python Coding Features

There are two ways to deal with the "entry point" for Python programs – one with a "main" function and one with unindented script starting on line one of a **.py** file. This book uses the simpler, unindented script *without* main.

The Python `input` function call may have text in its parentheses for its use prompt, like

```
age = input("How old are you?")
```

. But in this book, we begin by using a separate `print` statement for the prompt, followed by an `input` with empty parentheses. Doing so allows more flexibility in building prompts that contain variables, and in allowing user input to be either on the same line right *after* the prompt, or on the next line *under* the prompt. And it's a closer match to the console input sequences used in the C++ and Java books in this series. But the more common and concise way is used as well afterwards, where it makes sense to do so.

Python supports both “arrays” and “lists” as separate data structures. List elements behave more like Python variables, in that they are not “typed”, while Python’s array elements are typed. Also, Python arrays require an imported library, type restrictions, and don’t work with text – for example, you cannot have an array of names. So the array syntax used in this book is actually for Python lists, even though we refer to “arrays”.

Python supports for-loops for traversing collections without using indexes. But we stick to indexed for-loops to reinforce the concept of sequential storage in arrays, leaving other Python-specific code constructions to later studies of the Python language.

Table of Contents

PART 1: The Basics

Chapter 1. Programming Concepts

Programmers give instructions to computers in the form of "computer programs". Internet Explorer, Firefox, Word, Angry Birds, TurboTax, AutoCAD, etc., are all computer programs. They were developed by programmers and are used by other people to convert their typed, touched, spoken, clicked, and pasted input into some useful or entertaining form of output. The activity whereby programmers actually create computer programs is called "programming".

Programming involves three main steps: (1) understanding the problem to be solved, (2) writing computer "code" in a human-friendly computer language, and (3) translating the code into computer-readable form (like the 0's and 1's you see in science fiction movies). The *first step* is where human intelligence comes in – you certainly must understand something before you can explain it to someone else, like a computer. The *second step* involves using another computer program known as an "editor" to write in a computer language, like Basic, C, C++, C#, Java, PHP, Python, etc. The *last step* involves using *another* computer program (called an "interpreter" or "compiler") to translate code into something a computer can understand. In this book you will learn these three steps.

1.1 The First Step, Understanding

Alas, this is the part that new programming students tend to minimize and overlook. As a result, they end up being able to create very simple programs after a couple of months of study, but are unable to progress beyond that skill level. This happens because the first examples of programming and the first assignments are usually very easy problems (like "add two and two"), and to spend any time thinking how to solve such problems seems ludicrous. It's just easier to learn the mechanics of code editing and compiling without having to also devise solutions to complicated problems. So we tend to skip directly to the second step, code editing.

This works for a while, but eventually the problems get a bit harder (like "count the number of test scores that are above the average"). That's when we get stuck, because we never developed the habit of thinking, understanding, and planning *before* coding begins.

So here's a compromise: we will not focus on understanding at first, so as not to dismiss the concept due to its apparent irrelevance. But later on in this book, when the solutions to problems are no longer obvious, the discipline of understanding and planning will be reintroduced in the form of "algorithms".

1.2 Editors

An "editor" is a program used by programmers to write computer code. Code is a set of instructions that tells the computer how to collect input, process it, and express the results as output. These instructions are not exactly written in English, although they do resemble instruction sets that you may have seen in cooking (also known as "recipes") or after you buy something that has "some assembly required".

Code is written in a "computer language". Computer languages are *simplified* and *strict* versions of English. They are simplified in the sense that they include a *very small* subset of words from the English language, such as "if", "while", "for", "break", "continue", and only a hundred or so others. Computer languages are also strict in the sense that you have to say things and punctuate things *just right*, or the computer will not understand you. You even have to spell precisely, and use uppercase where you are supposed to, and use lowercase where you are supposed to, or the computer will not know what you are talking about! It takes *intelligence* to understand nuances of language, like accents, mispronunciations, incorrect choice of words, and misspellings – and remember that it's the *humans* who have the intelligence here, and not the computers.

There are three categories of editors that are typically used for programming, as explained below: general-purpose text editors, code editors, and IDE editors.

1.2.1 Text Editors

Using the vocabulary and grammar of a computer language, programmers type instructions in an editor. Any text editor will do, including Windows **Notepad**, UNIX or Linux **vi**, and Apple MacOSx **TextEdit**. These are *general-purpose text editors*, not specifically designed for use in coding, but they work fine.

Word, Pages, and other editors capable of "rich text formatting" are not very suitable for coding. They are page-oriented, and they embed formatting information into the files they produce. While it is possible to configure such editors for text editing, it is better to avoid them.

1.2.2 Code Editors

Code editors are special-purpose text editors created specifically for code editing. Code editors may include such useful features as code templates, line numbers, and syntax highlighting. Many code editors are available on the Internet for free download and installation, or for a reasonable price. Popular ones include **Notepad++**, **Bluefish**, **TextWrangler**, **Emacs**, **Crimson**, **jEdit**, **JNotePad**, to name a few.

1.2.3 IDEs

Finally there are the editors that are bundled with high-powered, interactive development environments, or "IDEs" for short. Python programmers often use products like **NetBeans**, **Aptana Studio**, **PyCharm**, and websites like repl.it. IDEs have some very useful features to help programmers, such as visual drag-and-drop development interfaces, and one-button run.

IDEs are the most complicated of the editor choices, and beginners really should avoid them. It's possible for an introductory computer course using an IDE to be too much about the tool at the expense of the subject: programming concepts. So while any editor choice is acceptable for use as you follow this book, the examples shown here use the Windows PC **NotePad** text editor and Apple Mac **TextEdit**.

1.3 Interpreters And Compilers

An "interpreter" is used by programmers to convert human-programmer-readable code into computer programs. They are sometimes also referred to as "compilers".

Python differs from the C++ and Java languages in that program execution is just a one-step. C++ and Java involve two steps – one to create a new version of the programmer's code and save it in a new file, and another step to execute *that* version of the program. Python does it all without an intermediate file.

In the C++/Java two-step process, any programming mistakes are caught in the first step, so by the time the second step gets done, those errors are worked out. In Python's one step, programming errors don't make themselves known until program execution reaches them.

1.4 Elements Of Computer Languages

Before you can type anything useful into an editor and save it to a file to be run later, you need to know some basics about computer languages. There are programming concepts that are common to all computer languages, and it would be nice to write an introductory book like this at the conceptual level instead of focusing on a specific language. But it is impractical to do so. We cannot get very far without typing some code, and that means choosing a language in which to work. Python is the language used in this book.

1.4.1 Statements And Expressions

A good way to explain the basic elements of computer languages is to compare them to the written English language. Text written in the English language consists of *sentences*; computer code consists of *statements*. While English sentences contain of *phrases*, computer statements contain of *expressions*.

In English	In Python
sentence: He is 21 years old.	*statement:* `age = 21`
phrase: over 30	*expression:* `age > 30`

In English, sentences are "read". In computer code, statements are "executed". Multiple English sentences follow one another vertically down a page. They are read in that order, and the development of thoughts depends on that order being followed. Similarly in computer code, multiple statements follow one another vertically down, and the processing of instructions depends on that order being followed. Long English sentences wrap to the next line down, and if there is still space on a line at the end of a sentence, the next sentence starts there. But wrapping is not generally used in code statements. And there is no concept of a "page". So statements in code are more like bullet points in English.

Calculating Area	
In English	**In Python 3**
• Measure the length.	`length = int(input("length="))`
• Measure the width.	`width = int(input("width="))`
• Multiply length and width, and save as area.	`area = length * width`
• Tell me the area.	`print("The area is", area)`

1.4.2 Sequential Processing

What's most important to understand at this point is the order in which statements are carried out. Think about giving someone driving directions – if they get the left- and right-turns out of order, they will probably end up lost! So in the above example, the statement that calculates area *must* come *after* the statements that collect values for length and width. Statements generally are not "learning experiences" for the computer. `area = length * width` is *not* telling the computer how to calculate the area of something. Instead it is an instruction that says to take the values currently stored as `length` and as `width`, multiply them, and save the result as `area`.

Below are examples of sequential processing presented as "recipes", in which numbered steps are processed from the top, down. Of course, we don't use the word "recipe" in computer programs – we call them "algorithms" instead:

Macaroni and Cheese
1 Preheat oven broiler.
2 Bring a large pot of water to a boil.
3 Add pasta to pot and cook 9 minutes.
4 Drain the pot.
5 Add pasta to a 2 qt dish.
6 Shred cheese and add to dish.
7 Add milk to dish.
8 Stir pasta, cheese, and milk in dish.
9 Microwave dish for 2 minutes.
10 Broil dish for 3 minutes.

Area Of A Room
1 Write labels "length" and "width" on paper.
2 Measure length of room, in decimal feet.
3 Write length on paper next to its label.
4 Measure width of room, in decimal feet.
5 Write width on paper next to its label.
6 Using a calculator, enter the length.
7 On the calculator, press **x**.
8 On the calculator, enter the width.
9 On the calculator, press **=**.
10 Write result on paper, with label "area".

This concept of sequential processing of statements is a key concept in programming.

1.4.3 Entry Point

The first statement to execute when a program starts is the "entry point" for the program. This seems like an obvious concept and not worthy of mention – isn't the first statement the one that appears on the first line of the code's file? Actually, it's not that easy. Come to think of it, it's not so easy in English either. In books, doesn't the first line of the first chapter usually come after the title page, the copyright page, and the preface and prologue? It's the same with coding. There are titles and prologues that come before the first statement. So when we get to actual code examples later, we will have to be aware that there will be prologue material, and there will have to be a way to identify the "entry point".

The next example adds some preparatory information at the top of the previous sequential processing example, to illustrate the concept of "entry point":

Macaroni and Cheese

INGREDIENTS
1 cup elbow macaroni pasta
1/4 cup milk
1-1/2 cups cheddar cheese

DIRECTIONS
entry point 1 Preheat oven broiler.
2 Bring a large pot of water to a boil.
3 Add pasta to pot and cook 9 minutes.
4 Drain the pot.
5 Add pasta to a 2 qt dish.
6 Shred cheese and add to dish.
7 Add milk to dish.
8 Stir pasta, cheese, and milk in dish.
9 Microwave dish for 2 minutes.
10 Broil dish for 3 minutes.

1.4.4 Branching And Looping

But starting at an entry point and executing every statement in sequential order does not provide enough flexibility for most purposes. What if the "width" is not entered correctly in the area-of-a-room example above? What if the person using the program types "ten" instead of "10"? What if they enter a negative number, or a number that is way higher than is reasonable? There should be a way to skip the calculation and provide the user with some... constructive feedback. Or what if the user has more than one area calculation to make? Should they have to restart the program again and again? Wouldn't it be better if the program started itself over automatically?

To accommodate these needs, computer programming includes the concepts of *branching* and *looping*. Branching enables one set of statements to be executed under some conditions, and another set under other conditions. This programming feature is illustrated with instructions to skip down (or *branch*) to a later statement. Looping enables a program to repeat itself. This programming feature is illustrated with instructions to skip up (or *loop back*) to a previous statement.

Here are some algorithm samples in which numbered steps are processed from the top, down:

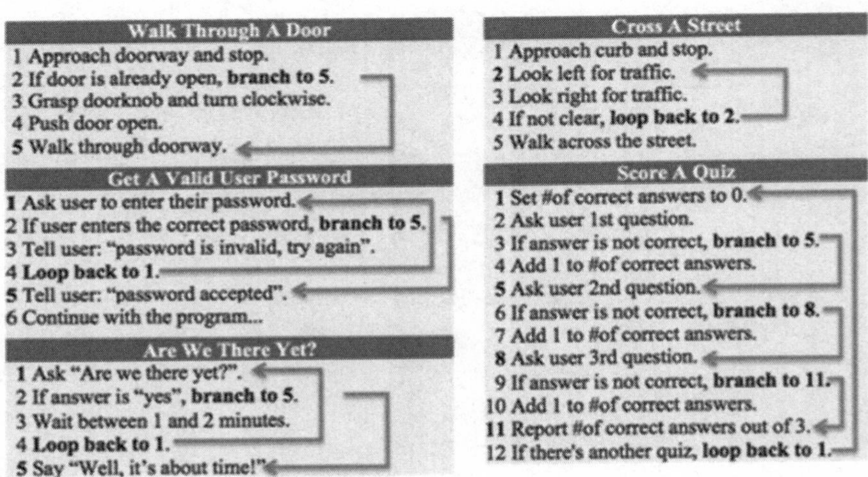

Study the examples provided above, and see if you can identify where *branching* is used, and where *looping* is used. After we gain enough skill to use sequential processing effectively in our programs, we will introduce the concepts of branching and looping. Look for this in the first chapter of Part 2.

1.4.5 Subprograms

For very complex programs it is convenient for the programmer to break down a large problem into several smaller problems – kind of a divide-and-conquer approach. Computer languages support the concept of subprograms. We do the same in the English language, when we provide details in web page links or in book appendices or Post-it notes.

For example, we will learn to write programs that ask the user for input. Our programs will "validate" the input (that is, make sure it is valid) before continuing with their processing. For invalid input, these programs will alert the user and offer another chance to enter valid input. As you can imagine, this involves a lot of detail – certainly some branching and looping will be included somewhere.

Here is an example that uses a subprogram to manage the details of the area calculation, using "jumps" between the main flow of the program and the subprogram, with lines and arrows showing the flow of the program:

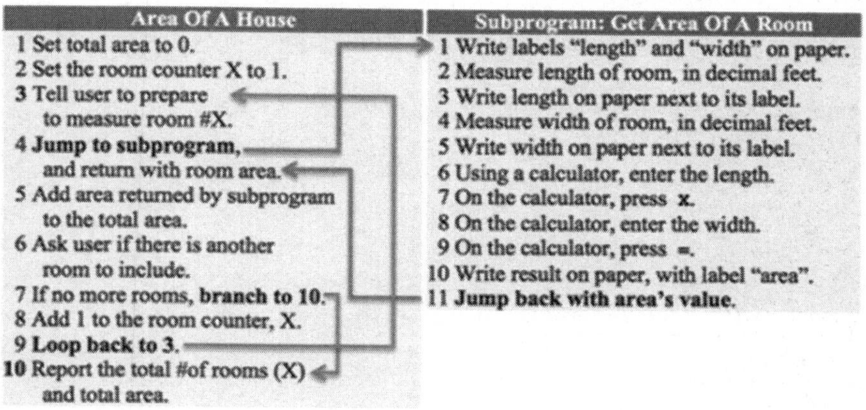

Area Of A House
1 Set total area to 0.
2 Set the room counter X to 1.
3 Tell user to prepare to measure room #X.
4 Jump to subprogram, and return with room area.
5 Add area returned by subprogram to the total area.
6 Ask user if there is another room to include.
7 If no more rooms, branch to 10.
8 Add 1 to the room counter, X.
9 Loop back to 3.
10 Report the total #of rooms (X) and total area.
Subprogram: Get Area Of A Room
1 Write labels "length" and "width" on paper.
2 Measure length of room, in decimal feet.
3 Write length on paper next to its label.
4 Measure width of room, in decimal feet.
5 Write width on paper next to its label.
6 Using a calculator, enter the length.
7 On the calculator, press x.
8 On the calculator, enter the width.
9 On the calculator, press =.
10 Write result on paper, with label "area".
11 Jump back with area's value.

The code for large programs can be obscured by the endless details of such simple operations. So detail is typically removed to subprograms (called "functions" in Python) and represented by a single statement directing the processing temporarily to the subprogram for the details of the operation. Look for this in the middle chapters of Part 2.

1.5 Exercises, Sample Code, Videos, And Addendums

Go to www.rdb3.com/python/1 for exercises that are suitable for lab assignments. They can be used exactly as they are, or copied, pasted, and marked up by instructors for use in their classes.

There are also some samples of solutions to other exercises to show students the format and detail they should expect to apply in solving the exercises. And there's a YouTube-like video, explaining the concepts presented in this chapter.

You'll find a similar URL at the end of each chapter of this book with extended information on the chapter's topic. New material gets added from time to time, especially in chapters where the details are affected by advances in technology, like chapter 2, which is about operating systems and Python software – technologies that change constantly.

Also, contributors are encouraged to send new materials to the author for possible inclusion in the chapter's extended information.

Chapter 2. Editing And Executing

Now that the main concepts of programming have been explained, it's time to actually do some programming. In order for you to edit and execute a program, you'll need a program to type, an editor, and Python. At first, what you will type will be provided for you – you'll type exactly what this book tells you to type. But as we move forward, you'll have more and more of an opportunity to write parts yourself, and ultimately write whole programs yourself.

Some of the instructions for editing and executing are "system-dependent" – that is, they depend on whether you are using a Windows PC or a Mac or something else. The presentation in this chapter is specific to Microsoft Windows on a PC and Apple OSX on a Mac. But where it's appropriate to do so, alternate instructions for UNIX/Linux are included.

Here's a checklist of the things you will need to consider:

Checklist
✓ **Choose an editor. Install, if necessary. Configure for your use.**
✓ **Choose a compiler. Install, if necessary. Configure for your use.**
✓ **Choose a folder on your system for storing your files.**
✓ **Configure your PC (if you are using Microsoft Windows)**

Once this checklist is completed, you will be ready to edit and run your first program in Python!

2.1 Choosing An Editor

The first thing to do is to choose an editor. Our choice for PCs is **Notepad**, which can be found under Start|All Programs|Accessories|Notepad. No installation is necessary for **Notepad**. Our choice for Mac is **TextEdit**, which can be found in Finder under Applications – also no installation.

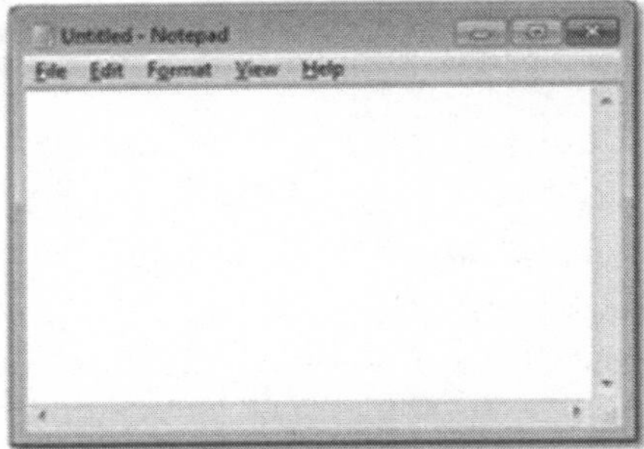

Notepad on a PC

TextEdit on a Mac

2.1.1 Configuring Notepad On A Windows PC

Two settings need to be made in **Notepad**, so that you can see "line numbers". The first is to turn off "word wrap" – to do so, use the Format menu. Make sure that there is no checkmark next to the "Word Wrap" option. If there is, click it to make it go away. Then turn on the "status bar". To do so, use the View menu. If there is a checkmark beside "Status Bar", leave it. Otherwise, click it. The Format and View menus should look like this when you're done:

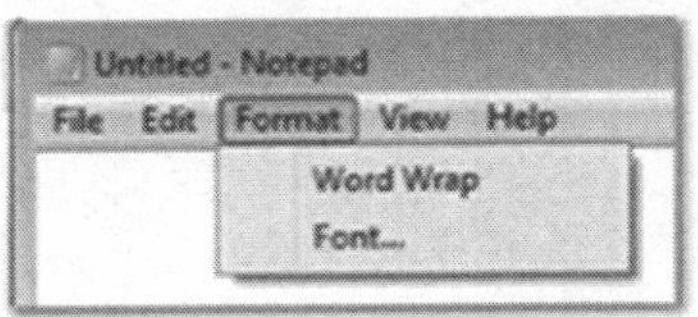

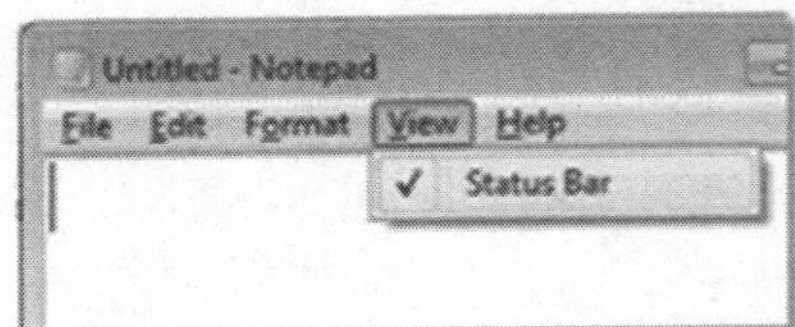

On your own computer these settings will persist from session to session. But in the computer lab, you probably will have to configure these each time you sit at a computer workstation.

2.1.2 Configuring TextEdit On A Mac

For Mac TextEdit, the default configuration is for "rich text". That will *not* do for programming. So go to the Format menu and click "Make Plain Text". Thereafter the menu will show "Make Rich Text" instead, and the edit window will look like the one on the right.

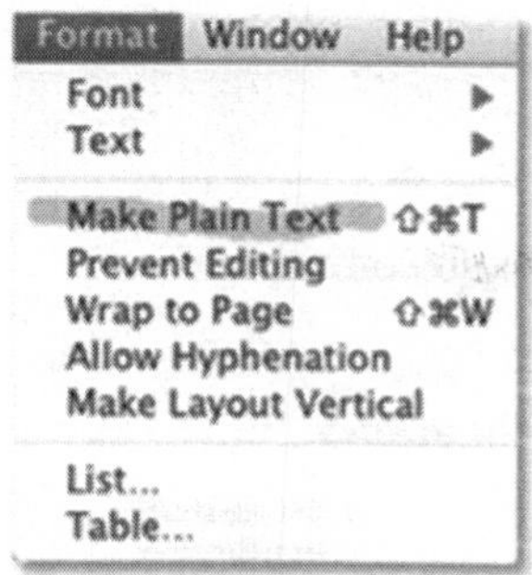

And this one is *really* important! Go to TextEdit's preferences and uncheck "Smart quotes" and "Smart dashes":

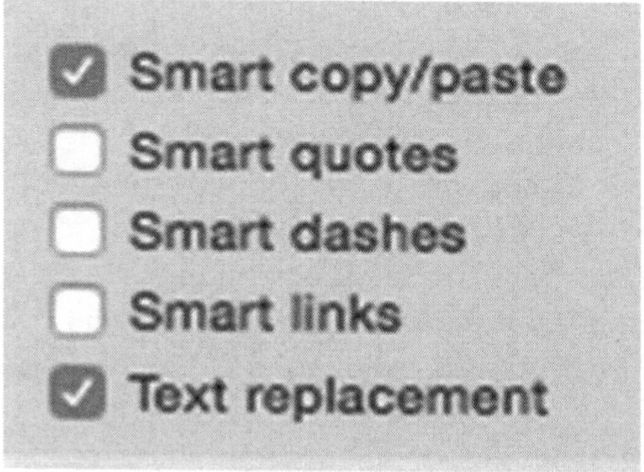

2.1.3 Installing JNotePad

The **JNotePad** editor was written by the author of this book. It is similar to **Notepad** and **TextEdit**, except that it works on almost any operating system, including Windows, OSX, and versions of Linux with a graphical user interface. It also contains menu-accessible Python (and C++ and Java) "code block" templates that match the examples in this book. Also, JNotePad is a good choice if you plan to go back and forth between a PC and a Mac, because it automatically deals with the extra blank lines and the loss of line breaks that happen with files that get traded back and forth between Macs and PCs. The JNotePad window looks like the one shown here.

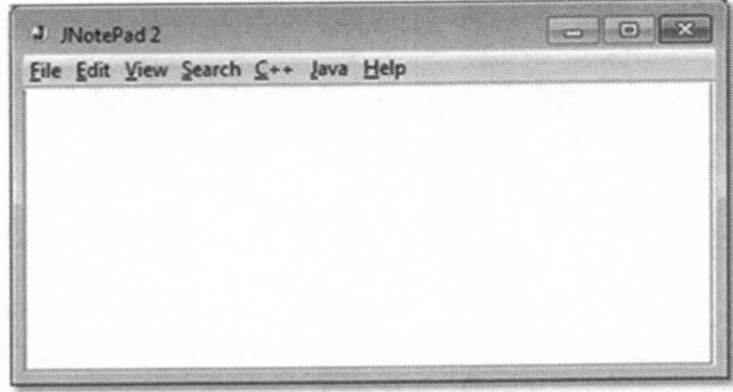

The installation of **JNotePad** is *very* easy – it just involves copying its startup icon from the Internet URL www.rdb3.com/jnotepad to your desktop or flash drive. Users of Mac computers can start using JNotePad right away for Python program editing. But in order for Windows PC users to use the icon, they first need to download and install either the "Java SE ***JRE***" or the "Java SE ***JDK***" from the Internet URL www.oracle.com/technetwork/java/javase/downloads, where the latest version at the time of this writing is Java SE 8u25. For Java compiling, you need the JDK, as explained below. The lighter JRE just for *running* programs that others (like yourself and like the author of JNotePad) wrote in Java.

2.2 Choosing Which Python To Use

There's more than one version of Python, and code written for one does not usually work in another without modification. For purposes of this book we use Python 3. Instructions for using Python on Windows PCs, Macs, Linux, and UNIX are presented below.

Actually, your system may already have Python installed. To find out if one is installed *and working* on your system, go to a "command prompt" and enter the command **`python -V`**.

2.2.1 What's A Command Prompt?

Just about all systems have a command prompt. It's a solid-color window (usually black or white) with a message (or "prompt") that indicates it's ready for a user to type a command. After a command gets typed, it gets sent to the system when the user presses the ENTER (or "return") key. Before we can talk about running a Python program, we need to get a command prompt so that we can type commands.

How you get to a command prompt depends on the system you're using. On a Mac, you simply run the Terminal app that is part of its OSX operating system – it's in the Applications folder. On Linux and UNIX systems, you probably start out with a command prompt when the computer boots up.

In Microsoft Windows there are lots of ways to get to a command prompt, so take your pick. One way is to use either the "run" or "search" option, and enter the three letters **cmd** – that should find a file named "cmd" or "cmd.exe", which you would then choose and run.

Another way is to look for the command prompt icon on the desktop or in the menu system, and click it.

If any of this works, you'll see something similar to this – a command prompt:

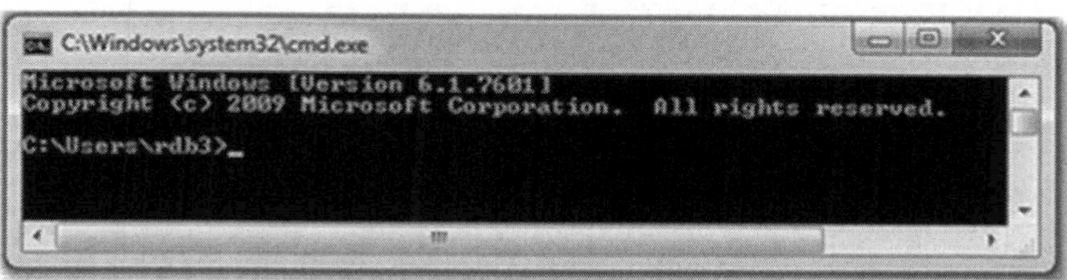

You'll be doing this so often that you may wish to "pin" its icon to the task bar.

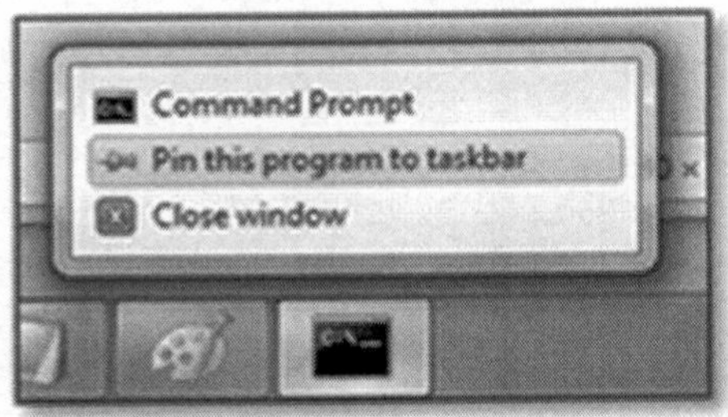

2.2.2 Maybe You Already Have Python

On your Windows PC, see if you have a folder on your "C" drive named "Python34". If so, see if there's a file there named **python** or **pythonw** or **python.exe**. If so, you have Python, and you can skip to the next section.

On your Mac, look in your Applications *folder* for something named "Python 3.4". If so, you have Python, and you can skip to the next section.

On any other system, go to a "command prompt" and enter the command `python -V` with an uppercase "V". If the reply is something like "Python 3.4.2", you're good. Anything with 3.4.something (or higher) is good.

Otherwise, you'll need to install Python 3.

Download and install from the Python download page, www.python.org/downloads, where the latest "3" version at the time of this writing is 3.4.3.

2.2.3 Configuring Python On A Windows PC

With Python installed on a Windows PC, it is important to confirm that it is in fact working correctly. Even if you found it was already installed, it is still important to perform the same confirmation steps as if you yourself installed it.

In order to use Python, you need to type some configuration commands. First confirm that you have a folder named **C:\Python34** or something similar. Note that there may be a different name for the **Python34** folder on your Windows system. You may even have more than one installation. If so, pick the latest one. Once you determine the folder name for your system, modify the following instructions to use that folder name instead of **Python34**.

To begin a Python programming session using command-line compiling, open a command prompt. Here's what it should look like (in Windows XP and 8):

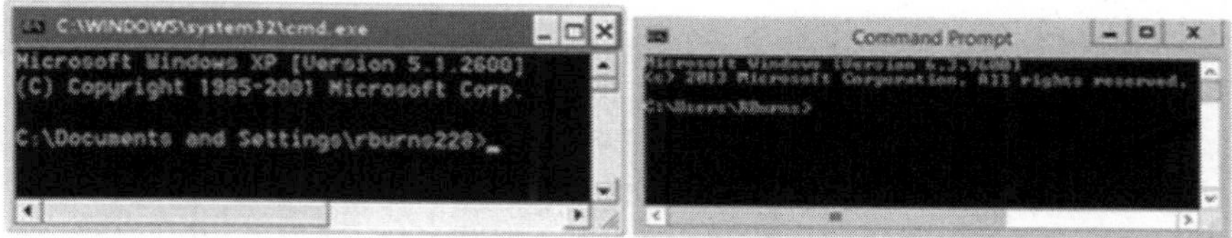

Every time you begin a Python session, you *may* have to enter this command: **path=c:\Python34;%path%**. If yours works without it, great!

There is no feedback or other output produced by the `path` command, but the `python -V` command should report "version 3", like this:

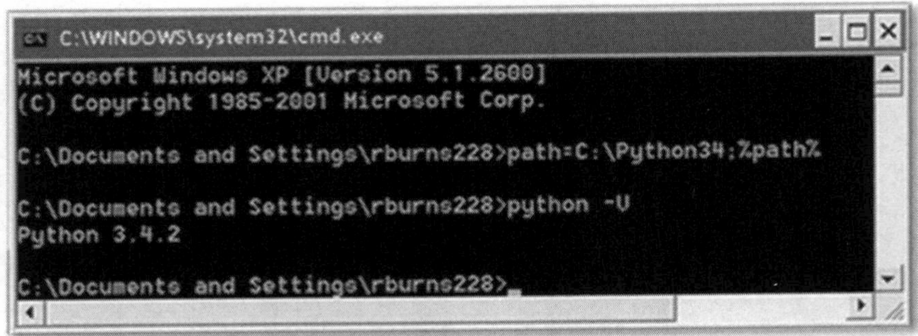

2.2.4 Configuring Python On A Mac

Once Python is installed on a Mac, it is important to confirm that it is in fact working correctly and that you're using Python 3.

To begin a Python programming session using command-line compiling, launch the Terminal app, and you should see a window appear on your desktop:

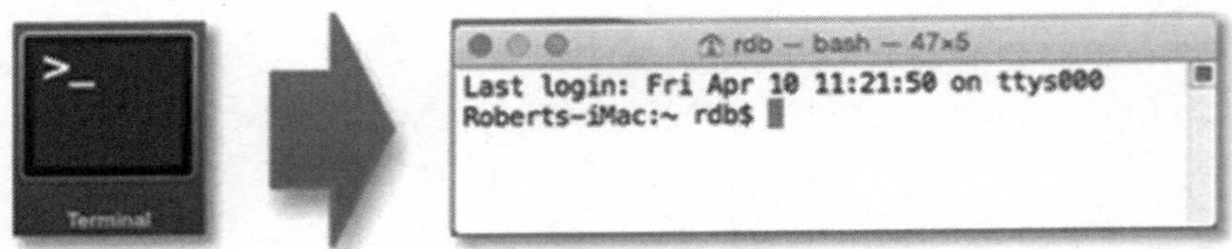

The `python -V` command should work, but if it says version 2, then try the command `python3 -V`. If that works, then do this:

Every time you begin a Python session, enter this command: `alias python='python3'`. Then proceed as normal – you're running Python 3! Or you can just use the command `python3` instead of `python` to run your Python programs.

```
rdb — bash — 47×10
Last login: Thu Apr  9 16:00:06 on ttys000
Roberts-iMac:~ rdb$ python -V
Python 2.7.6
Roberts-iMac:~ rdb$ python3 -V
Python 3.4.2
Roberts-iMac:~ rdb$ alias python='python3'
Roberts-iMac:~ rdb$ python -V
Python 3.4.2
Roberts-iMac:~ rdb$
```

2.2.5 Using Python Online

You can also use Python fully online through free websites like repl.it, tutorialspoint.com, and ideone.com. You can edit and execute code directly in your favorite browser! While you ultimately may not decide to rely on these for your programming assignments, they do offer handy access to Python when you need it.

2.3 Choosing A Folder For Storing Files

To store your Python "source files" on a PC or Mac and do your programming work, you should have a folder reserved specifically for that purpose. This is called your "working folder". Decide upon this and get it ready *before* writing your first program.

You can put your working folder on a hard drive or on removable media, like a flash drive. If you are not yet comfortable with "command line" mode or file structure navigation, it's easiest to simply use a flash drive or a cloud folder. Also, with your files on a flash drive they are readily portable between home and classroom and lab, and so on – even between PC and Mac. The rest of this section is organized for students using flash drives, as others with more experience can easily adapt the instructions for themselves.

On a PC, use Windows Explorer to create your working folder on your flash drive. On a Mac, your flash drive icon should already appear on your desktop with a default name, like "NO NAME". You can rename it as you would rename any file or folder on your Mac desktop. It's better to name it *without spaces* – something like **programming**, and thereafter it will appear on your desktop like this:

Now create your working folder on your flash drive, named for example, **python**. While it's possible to put this folder inside some other folder on the flash drive, the rest of this section is written as though the working folder is *not* inside some other folder.

Next, figure out how to locate your working folder in command line mode. On a PC, open a command prompt window as explained previously. Navigate to your flash drive by typing the letter designation of the drive, then a colon, and then press ENTER. That is, enter the command **j:** if your flash drive designation is "J". Then navigate to your working folder using a command like **cd\python**, for example.

On a Mac, start the Terminal app and enter the command **cd /volumes/programming/python**, for example. That's **cd**, not **CD**, and it's slash **/**, not backslash ****. And don't forget the space after **cd** on the Mac.

Or on either Mac or PC, type **cd** , drag and drop your working folder onto it, and press ENTER. That's c d *space*, not just c d. Then you can do the drag and drop to complete the command, and then press ENTER.

2.3.1 How To Backup Your Files

The rule is simple: "only backup the files that you do not want to lose." After you finish editing your source files, and save them onto a hard drive or flash drive, imagine for a moment what would happen if the hard drive fails tonight or you misplace your flash drive. It's a good idea to backup your files by putting a copy of them on the Internet. There are several free options, including emailing attachments to yourself, and file hosting services like Dropbox and Google Drive. If you are doing assignments for a computer course you are taking, the course may even offer a class website for submitting your files, and you could use that to backup your work.

Decide on your own process for backing up your work, and make it a habit to email or upload your files at the end of each work session.

2.4 Configuring A Windows PC For Programming

Actually, you can use PCs for programming without any configuration changes. But there is one change that makes things easier for identifying files, and it is *highly* recommended. The problem is that Windows hides filename extensions by default. That is, a program's file **hello.py** may appear only partially – that is, without the dot and the "py" after the dot – in a file listing. To change this behavior, start **Windows Explorer** from its icon, which looks like this in Windows 8:

Then use the menu command "Organize|Folder and Search Options". Click the "View" tab, and remove the checkmark from "Hide extensions for known file types".

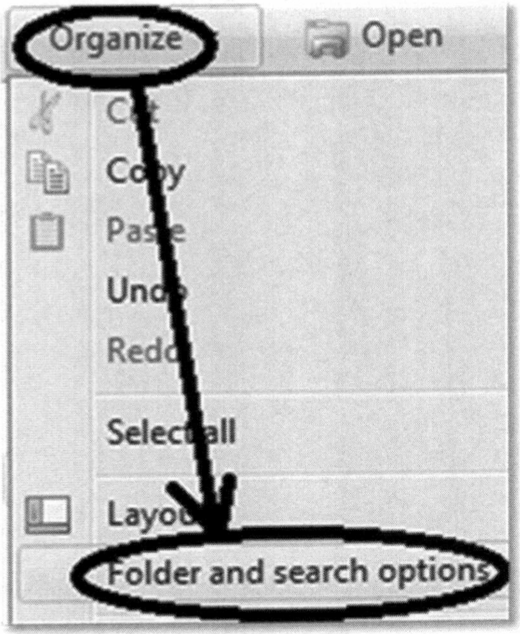
Organize
Open
Folder and search options

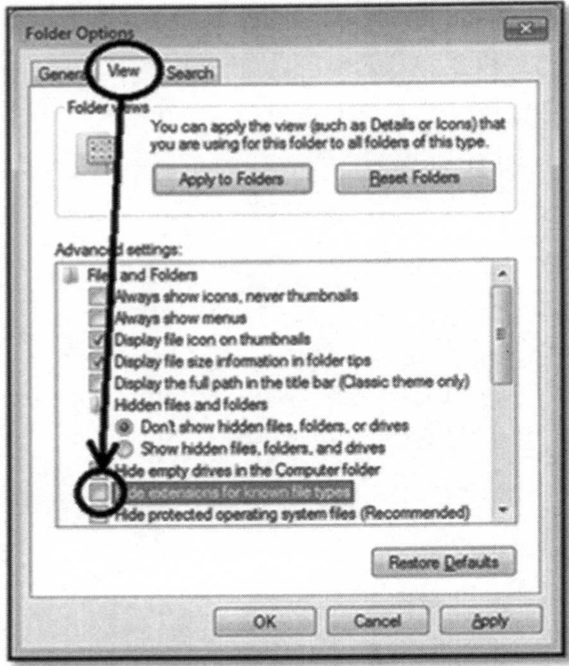
Folder Options
Search
You can apply the view (such as Details or Icons) that you are using for this folder to all folders of this type.
Apply to Folders
Reset Folders
Always show icons, never thumbnails
Always show menus
Display file icon on thumbnails
Display file size information in folder tips
Display the full path in the title bar (Classic theme only)
Hidden files and folders
Don't show hidden files, folders, or drives
Show hidden files, folders, and drives
Hide empty drives in the Computer folder
Hide protected operating system files (Recommended)
Restore Defaults
OK
Cancel
Apply

The Windows 7 folder options are also located in the Control Panel, under Appearance and Personalization. Look for Folder Options, then the View tab, and then uncheck "Hide extensions for known file types". Click OK and then close.

On your own computer, this setting will persist from session to session. But in a computer lab, you may have to configure this each time. Note that Macs do not hide filename extensions, so no configuration is necessary.

2.5 Editing

Okay – we are ready to program! Let's start by writing the world's smallest Python program, and compiling and running that. It actually doesn't do anything, but if you are able to get this far, then you can at least establish that you can use an editor and that you have Python. With these details out of the way, we can focus on learning to program! Here's our first program:

World's Smallest Python Program (well, almost)

```
print("Hello")
```

Start up your text editor. The examples in this book are shown in Windows **Notepad**, but you can use any other editor and system. So if you are using Mac, you can use **TextEdit**, configured for plain text. And if you are using Linux or UNIX, use **vi** or any other text editor with which you are familiar.

Note that the line is fully left justified. That is *very important* in Python. Python does not use "curly-braces" like many other languages do, so how lines are indented or not indented does in Python what curly-braces do in other languages.

2.5.1 How To Type Code

The tendency is to type code "linearly" – that is, from the top line to the bottom, from left to right. But that is not the best way to type code. Matching parentheses and quotes and levels of indent appear throughout code. The toughest part is to keep track of these and make sure that each open parenthesis has a matching closing parenthesis, etc. The easiest way to do that is to type opening and closing symbols together, and then separate them.

In the "World's Smallest Python Program" above, you should type **print**, then the opening parenthesis followed *immediately* by its matching closing parenthesis. Then put your edit cursor between the parentheses and type two quote marks (as a container for the word hello). Then put your edit cursor between the quote marks and type **Hello**.

Note that as you type the program, there is an indication on the editor about the line number that is currently being edited. In **Notepad** this is located in the lower right with the abbreviations "Ln" for line number and "Col" for column number. (If this does not appear, then revisit section 2.1.1 above.) This is not so important for now, but knowing the line number will be important when we get into larger programs, in case Python detects and reports typing errors. Unfortunately the line number does not appear in TextEdit on a Mac – one reason why JNotePad may be the better choice for an editor.

2.5.2 Saving A File

Save the file as **hello.py**, into the "working folder" you created for storing your programming files (**j:\python** on a PC in the examples in this book). If you use **Notepad** on a PC, you may have to enclose the filename in quotes, or else **.txt** may be appended to the filename! The saved file is called the "source file", and it contains "source code". It should look something like this on PCs and Macs:

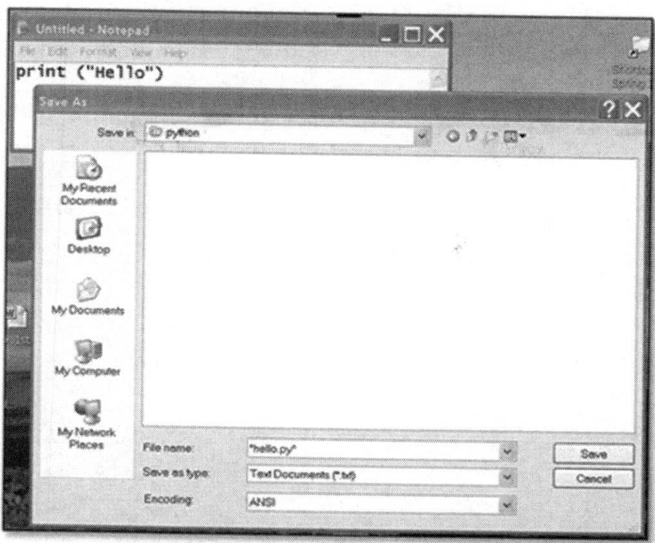
Untitled - Notepad
print ("Hello")
Save As
Save in: python
My Recent Documents
Desktop
My Documents
My Computer
My Network Places
File name: "hello.py"
Save as type: Text Documents (*.txt)
Encoding: ANSI
Save
Cancel

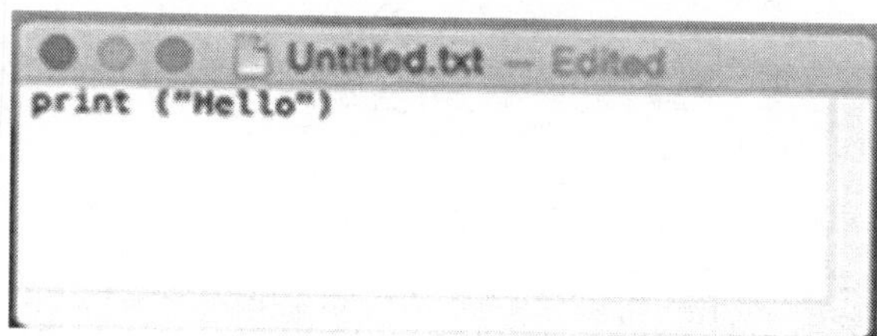
Untitled.txt — Edited
print ("Hello")

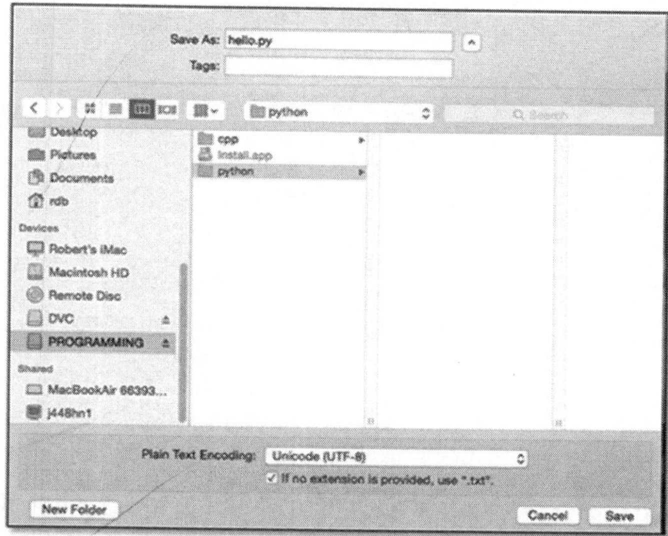
Save As: hello.py
Tags:
python
Desktop
Pictures
Documents
rdb
Devices
Robert's iMac
Macintosh HD
Remote Disc
DVC
PROGRAMMING
Shared
MacBookAir 66393...
j448hn1
cpp
Install.app
python
Plain Text Encoding: Unicode (UTF-8)
If no extension is provided, use ".txt".
New Folder
Cancel
Save

2.6 Executing (Or "Running")

Now that the program's source file has been saved to the drive, you are ready to execute it, or as it's also called, "run". The two words are used interchangeably in programming.

First, go to a command prompt as explained above, and navigate to the drive and working folder containing your edited source file. It should look like this on a PC or Mac, with what *you* would type appearing like this: `cd\python` in the PC screen shots, and like this: `cd /Volumes/programming/python` in the Mac screenshots:

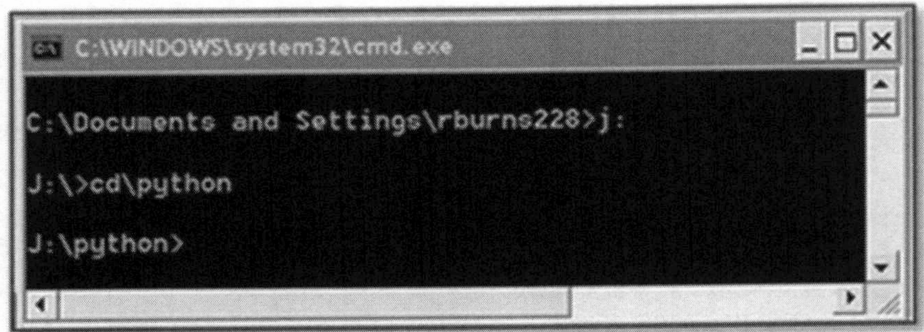

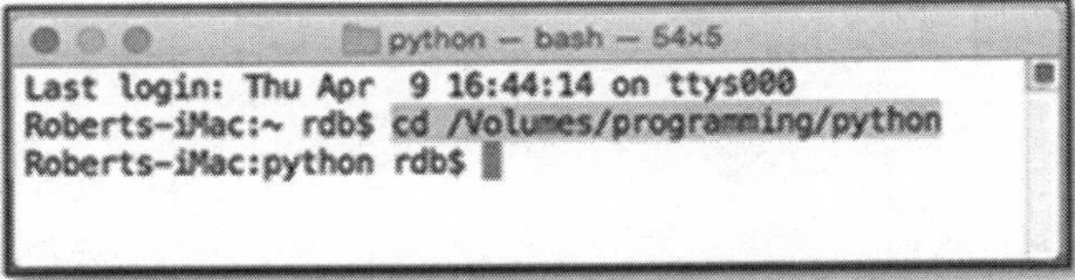

2.6.1 How To Execute

Here's how to ***EXECUTE*** it. Invoke Python by typing this command:

```
python hello.py
```

```
python — bash — 53x7
Last login: Thu Apr  9 17:00:10 on ttys000
Roberts-iMac:~ rdb$ alias python='python3'
Roberts-iMac:~ rdb$ cd /Volumes/programming/python
Roberts-iMac:python rdb$ python hello.py
Hello
Roberts-iMac:python rdb$
```

If there are any errors, it should be evident from the output. Line numbers should also appear in Python's output, guiding you to the problem, like this (with a missing quote mark):

```
Roberts-iMac:python rdb$ python hello.py
  File "hello.py", line 1
    print ("Hello)
                 ^
SyntaxError: EOL while scanning string literal
Roberts-iMac:python rdb$
```

2.6.2 Rerunning

When you use the command line to run your programs, it will seem as if there is a lot of typing to do – repetitive typing. But you do not have to retype a command over and over again. PCs and Macs both let you use the UP and DOWN ARROWs of the keyboard to recall a recently typed command. On PCs, you can also use the F7 key to get a menu of recently typed commands, although the UP ARROW is the easiest way to recall the last-typed command.

2.7 Exercises, Sample Code, Videos, And Addendums

Go to www.rdb3.com/python/2 for extended materials pertaining to this chapter.

Chapter 3. Values, Variables, And Calculations

Make sure that you have figured out the steps for editing and saving source files and that you can execute your programs before proceeding with this chapter. You may change your choice of systems (PC or Mac or online) or editors during your study, and that's okay. It's good for a computer programmer to work independent of any specific system or editor. But for now, find something that works for you and try to stick with it as you go through the first part of this book.

Now that you have figured out how to create computer programs in Python, let's do something a bit more interesting. This section introduces the concepts of data "values", "variables" for storing data values, and "calculations" for processing data. It covers the three parts of simple programs: assigning input values, performing calculations using those values, and displaying output. The techniques explained in this chapter will enable you to write programs that can do calculations like Excel spreadsheets can do.

3.1 Values

A "value" is a piece of information used in a computer program. Values can be combined in such simple operations as addition, or processed in more complicated operations like spell checking. Values can be specified by the programmer, entered by a user, or read from a disk file – all of which are covered in this book. There are two distinct types of values used in computer programs: *numbers* and *text* (or words).

The ways in which computers remember, process, and display data values depends on whether the values are numeric or text. It's as if computers had "left brain/right brain" separation, which is the concept that we humans process logic with the left side of our brains and emotion with the right side. Similarly, computers have one way of "thinking about" numbers, and another way for text. So in computer programming, for each step that involves data values of some kind, the computer has to be "told" that "we're working with numbers now", or "get ready to handle some text".

Actually, it gets a bit more specific in Python programming, because not only is there a distinction between numbers and text, there are finer distinctions for numbers. Numbers can be either whole numbers, as might be used in counting (like 1, 2, 3, etc.), or they can allow fractional or decimal parts, as might be used to record grade point average (for example, 3.24) or temperature (like 98.6 degrees F).

You might wonder why we would even bother with this. Can't the fractional or decimal part of a value be zero? So why have special categories for whole numbers? The reason is that there are certain efficiencies in the ways that computers deal with the simpler forms of numbers. The simplest numbers are whole numbers. So in dealing with numeric values, if we can use elements of the computer language that are intended for whole numbers, we do so. Otherwise we use the more general ways of dealing with numbers that may or may not have fractional parts.

Unlike C++ and Java, there's no special distinction for single-character text in Python.

3.2 Variables

A "variable" is something in a computer program that programmers use to store a value. People can remember values by writing them on paper – computers use "variables". Sometimes data values are specified in a program's code, written there by the *programmer*. Other times the source of the data value is input, as from a keyboard or text file (as we will study in chapters 5 and 10 of this book), allowing a *user* of the program to specify them. Still other times the source is the result of a calculation made in the program, such as calculating area based on length and width, and using that to calculate how much paint to buy. In any case, variables are simply the things that store data values in a computer program.

3.2.1 Identifiers

Variables have names, or "identifiers". On paper, people might write labels or other descriptions by the values they write, so they remember what the values mean. Computers use "identifiers" to do the same thing. By referring to the name of a variable in a computer program, its associated data can be stored or retrieved. The memory used by variables is typically recyclable – that is, you can store a new value in a variable (after you are finished with the old value, of course). Similarly, people can cross out or erase previously written values and write new ones, like keeping score of a ball game.

Variable names are chosen by the programmer, who can select just about anything. But there are some *rules*: the name must consist of one or more lowercase letters, uppercase letters, digits, and/or underscore symbols – no spaces are allowed! Also, the name may not begin with a digit, and it cannot be the same as one of the hundred or so words used in the language (called "keywords"), such as "if" and "while". For example, `age` could be used for a variable that stores a person's age.

Besides the rules, there are some *conventions* which most programmers follow: variables usually begin with a lowercase letter. Also, identifiers consisting of more than one word, since they cannot be separated by spaces, are run together with the first character in each word after the first being uppercase. For example, `firstName` could be used for a variable that stores a person's first name.

The number of variables that a programmer can use in a program is basically limited by the amount of memory in the computer. For today's desktop computers, notebooks, tablets, and smart phones, it is *practically* unlimited.

3.2.2 Declaration Statements

So for each item of data to be stored, there needs to be a variable. To create a variable in a Python program, you have to specify two things: a unique identifier for the variable, and an initial value to store in the variable. It's that initial value that informs the variable about *the type of data* the variable's supposed to store.

This specification must be made as a *statement*, and it is called a "declaration statement". To reserve memory to store a numeric value in a variable named "age", it looks something like this:

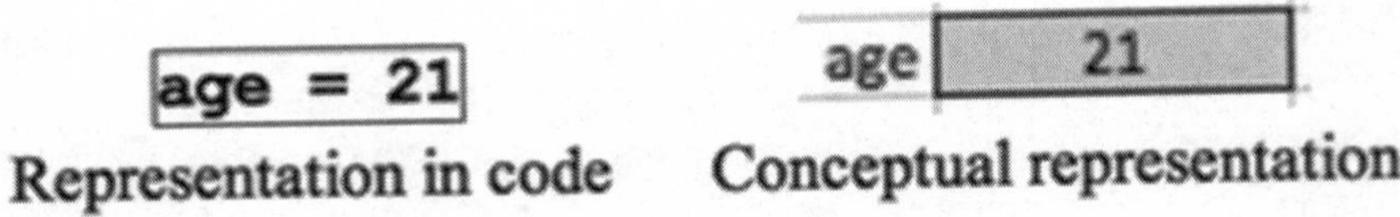

If you're used to C++ or Java, note that a semicolon is *not* required at the end of a Python statement. But it is allowable, and some programmers do use semicolons to mark the end of statements. We'll not be using them in this book.

To declare a variable for storing text, you could use a statement like `firstName = "George"` as in the following program – note the left justification, aligning the four lines of code so that the first letters of their identifiers are all directly under one another:

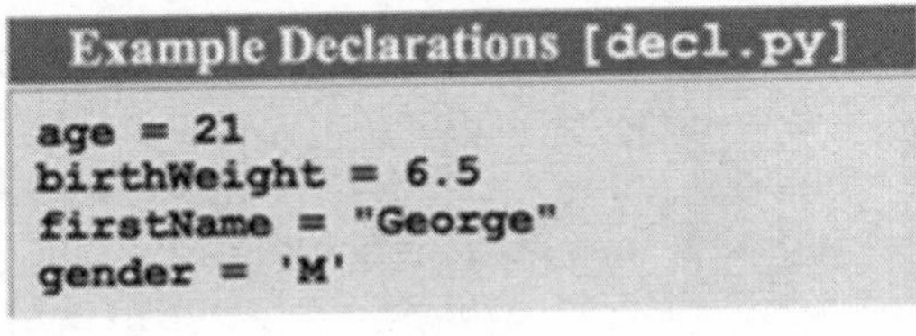
Example Declarations [decl.py]

```
age = 21
birthWeight = 6.5
firstName = "George"
gender = 'M'
```

what goes on in memory:

age	21
birthWeight	6.5
firstName	"George"
gender	'M'

Note also that:

- Spaces surround the "equals" sign – they are not required, but they make the code easier for humans to read.
- One text value is set off in double quotes and the other in single quotes. These are interchangeable in Python. You can use either, as long as the opening symbol matches the closing symbol.

In Python, you *cannot* use a variable in a calculation or in output until it's been declared. If you try, an error occurs when it reaches that statement during execution, and the output explains that you tried to use a variable before it was "defined".

3.2.3 Assignment Statements

To change a value *after* a variable's declaration, use a statement like `age = 22` It looks *exactly the same* as the original declaration statement, so in Python it's really important to spell *and case* the variable's identifier the same assignment statements, or else you end up declaring another, different variable. For example, doing `Age = 22` creates a new variable, leaving the original `age` at 21.

3.3 Calculations

Once variables have been declared with proper values assigned, they can be considered as inputs to calculations. Calculations take place in *expressions*, which usually involve variables, numbers, and an *operation symbol*, like a plus sign. For example, `a + b` is an expression that results in adding the values stored in 2 variables, named "a" and "b". Note that for this expression to be valid, both `a` and `b` must have been declared with values *before* the expression appears. In these examples, `a` and `b` must have been assigned *numeric* values. (We'll get into text expressions later.)

In an expression like `a + b`, the `a` and `b` are called "operands". An operand in a calculation expression can be a variable name, as shown in the examples so far, or they can be values. For example, `10 + 17`, `a + 5`, or `7 + b`, are all valid calculation expressions, or "math operations".

Some other simple math operations besides addition are subtraction (`a - b`), multiplication (`a * b`), and division (`a / b`). There's "whole number division", where any remaining fraction is discarded (`a // b`). There is also modulus (`a % b`) which results in *only* the remainder of an whole number division problem "b goes into a... with the remainder...". You know how to use addition, subtraction, multiplication, and division. Here's how some of these work:

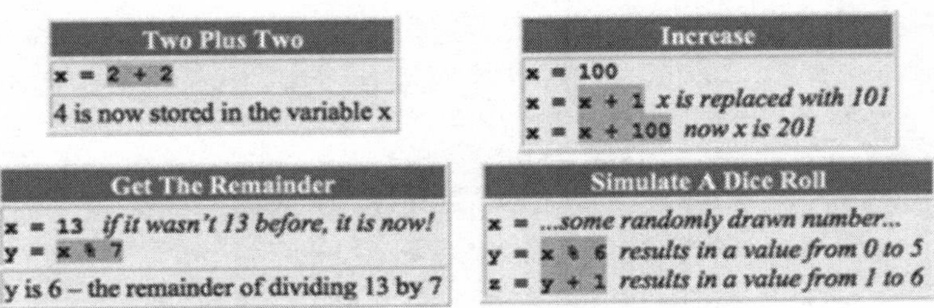

Calculation expressions can have numbers as operands as well as variables, like `a / 3` and `2 + 2`. They almost always involve two values and an operation symbol in between.

3.3.1 Using Calculation Expressions In Statements

Remember that expressions do not stand alone – they have to be used in statements. In the same way, words in English do not stand alone – they need to be used in sentences in order to be understood in the proper context. The simplest way to use a calculation expression in a statement is to use it in an *assignment statement*. For example, `c = a + b`. This statement performs the addition of "a" and "b", and stores the result in the variable named "c", either declaring "c" as a new variable, or reusing a previously declared "c" by overwriting what was there before.

Note that the equal sign in the assignment statement is *not* the same as the equal sign in mathematics! In math it is used to express equivalence between the two sides of the equal sign. In programming, it means to evaluate the expression on the *right side* of the equal sign, and store the result in the variable on the *left* side of the equal sign. It does *not* establish equivalence for the computer to remember and apply where appropriate – remember: sequential processing! You *usually* don't put anything except for a single variable on the left side.

Look at the counting application below and see if you can understand what is going on.

An Application: Counting

`total = 0` *stores 0 in variable "total"*
`total = total + 1` *replaces 0 with 0+1, or 1*
`total = total + 1` *replaces 1 with 1+1, or 2*

Note that it involves *replacing* what is stored in the declared variable. Variables can remember multiple values in a program, but only one of them at a time. The statement `total = total + 1` reads like this: "Retrieve what is stored in `total` and add `1` to it. Then store the result in `total`, replacing what was there". In assignment statements, resolve what is on the *right-hand side of the equal sign* first, and then store the resulting value in the variable that appears on the *left-hand side of the equal sign.* Never put anything other than a single variable's name to the left of the equal sign, as you see in all the above examples.

3.3.2 Complex Expressions

Math operations in computer languages involve 2 values. But we often have to solve problems with more than 2 values, such as the average of 3 numbers. So how is that done using programming languages? First realize that the averaging of 3 numbers is really a series of 2-value operations. Add the first and second numbers together. Then add the third number. Finally, divide by three. Calculators work this way – do an operation with 2 numbers, then use that result as the first number in the next 2-value operation, and so on. Multiple-step calculations can be done by breaking them down into steps involving only two values. So we can write this in a series of statements, or we can use complex expressions that let us combine a series of 2-value expressions into a single statement. Here are three ways to find the average of 3 numbers:

Using Simple Expressions

```
age1 = 19
age2 = 21
age3 = 30

averageAge = age1 + age2
averageAge = averageAge + age3
averageAge = averageAge / 3
```

Using Complex Expressions

```
age1 = 19
age2 = 21
age3 = 30

averageAge = ((age1 + age2) + age3) / 3
                ...or...
averageAge = (age1 + age2 + age3) / 3
```

Using Simple Expressions

```
age1 = 19
age2 = 21
age3 = 30

averageAge = age1 + age2
averageAge = averageAge + age3
averageAge = averageAge / 3
```

Using Complex Expressions

```
age1 = 19
age2 = 21
age3 = 30

averageAge = ((age1 + age2) + age3) / 3
                ...or...
averageAge = (age1 + age2 + age3) / 3
```

In the simple expressions solution, note the statement `averageAge = averageAge + age3`. This is a kind of assignment statement that will *overwrite* an existing value with a new value. Remember that data stored in memory can be replaced when it is no longer needed.

The parentheses (in the solution with complex expressions) enclose and isolate one 2-value operation, so that it can be completed and the result *substituted* into the remaining expression. So `((age1 + age2) + age3) / 3` resolves to `((19 + 21) + age3) / 3` resolves to `(40 + age3) / 3` resolves to `(40 + 30) / 3` resolves to `70 / 3`, etc.

Actually it is acceptable to write this as `(age1 + age2 + age3) / 3`, because computer languages treat multiple successive additions as though they were paired in parentheses. But it's *not* okay to write it as `age1 + age2 + age3 / 3`, because that mixes addition and multiplication. In such cases, the multiplications (and divisions) are done first in the order in which they appear, left to right. Then the additions (and subtractions) are done. So `age3 / 3` would be evaluated first, then `age1 + age2`, etc.

3.3.3 Manipulating Text

So far all of the calculations have involved numbers, since that's usually what we think of when we apply math operations like addition. But Python also support text. Are there operations that are meaningful for those?

Actually, text can be manipulated in several ways using Python. Text stored in two separate variables can be combined, one after the other – this is called "concatenation". Text operations can be done on text variables with any other text variable or text value.

For example, consider the declared text variable `s = "Hello"`. The expression `s + "World"` *joins* two text values – the result is HelloWorld, without a separating space. For there to be a space, the expression would have to be `s + " World"` or `s + " " + "World"` instead.

Another manipulation of text is getting its size by counting the number of letters (and spaces and punctuation) in the text. The expression is `len(s)`, which returns as a whole number the size of the text variable `s`.

And here's another. The expression is `s[2]` returns the character at position 2 in the text variable `s`. Position counting is "zero-based", so `s[2]` returns the first "l" in Hello, not the "e".

Here's an example using text manipulation to create a "form letter":

Example: A Form Letter [formLetter.py]

```
name = "George Washington"
s = "Congratulations, "
s = s + name
s = s + "! You have been selected to"
s = s + " receive one of 5 valuable prizes!"
```

The above program does not actually produce any *output* – it just builds and stores a text value. In order to get a program to produce output, we have to include "output statements", which are introduced next. And then we have to "execute" the program on the command line.

3.4 Output

By now we can store data, perform calculations, and manipulate text. But without output statements, the program keeps all of this to itself! This section explains how to show output on the console screen.

The Python output statement is `print()`. Any expression, variable, or number that you put inside the parentheses will appear on the display monitor, below the command that executes your program.

Here are the averaging and form letter examples from above, with output added:

Complete Example: Average Age [age.py]

```
age1 = 19
age2 = 21
age3 = 30

averageAge = age1 + age2
averageAge = averageAge + age3
averageAge = averageAge / 3

print("The average age is", averageAge)
```

Complete Example: Form Letter [formLetter2.py]

```
name = "George Washington"
s = "Congratulations, "
s = s + name
s = s + "! You have been selected"
s = s + " to receive one of 5"
s = s + " valuable prizes!"
print(s)
```

3.4.1 Showing Variables' Values On The Console Screen, *With Labels*

Programmers usually do not output just a variable's value all by itself, like this:

```
print(age)
```

...because it is difficult to read and understand it on the console screen. In this case, the output could be something like "21" – how does the user of your program know what "21" means, especially if the values of other variables are also shown?

It is better to label your output, so that it looks something like this: "my age is 21" instead of just "21". To include a label in an output statement with one variable, use a statement like this:

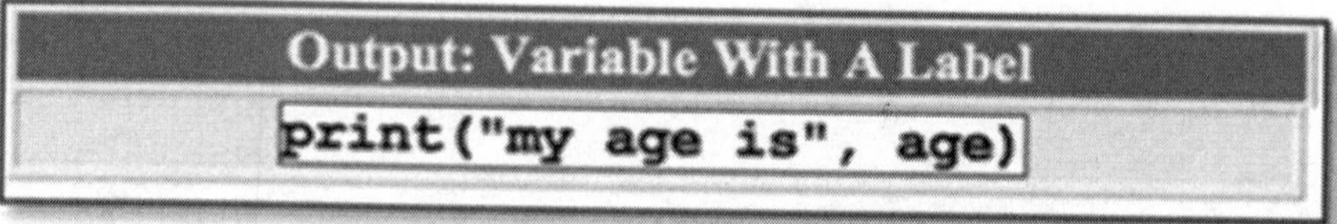

Output: Variable With A Label
print("my age is", age)

You can put as many things as you want in a print statement's parentheses, separated by commas. Python automatically separates them with spaces – whether you want it to or not! Spaces after the commas do nothing except make the print statement more readable for humans.

When sending a variable's value to the console screen, be sure to put the *variable's name* in the output statement. Do *not* put its *value*. For example:

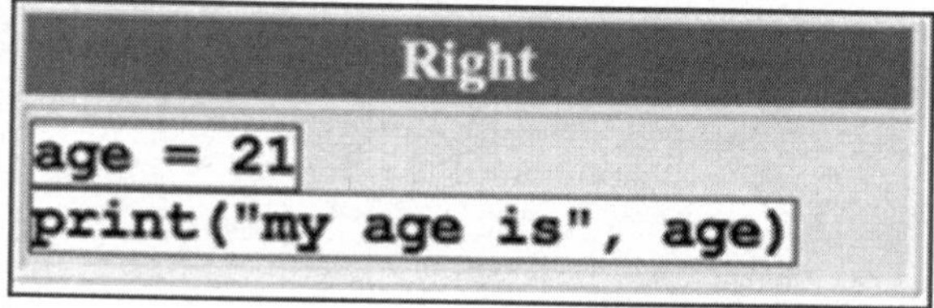

Right
age = 21
print("my age is", age)

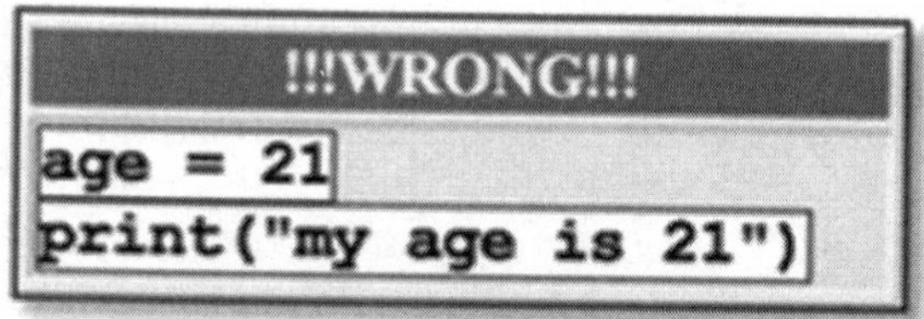

!!!WRONG!!!
age = 21
print("my age is 21")

Yes, both result in the same output, but from a maintenance standpoint, the "wrong" way is more difficult to maintain. For example, if you want to change the program next year so that it outputs "22", you would have to change it every place it appears in your program, and each change offers an opportunity for a typing error. But in the "right" way, you just change "21" to "22" in one place, and rest of the program picks up the change automatically and reliably.

3.4.2 A Complete Example: Variable, Values, And Calculations

Here is a program that takes a recipe for one cup of hot chocolate, and multiplies it to serve 8:

Complete Example: Recipe Ingredients Converter [hotChocolate.py]

```
cupsOfMilk = 0.83;
vanillaBeans = 0.25;
cinnamonSticks = 0.5;
ouncesOfChocolate = 0.75;

iWantThisManyCups = 8;

cupsOfMilk = cupsOfMilk * iWantThisManyCups;
vanillaBeans = vanillaBeans * iWantThisManyCups;
cinnamonSticks = cinnamonSticks * iWantThisManyCups;
ouncesOfChocolate = ouncesOfChocolate * iWantThisManyCups;

print()
print("Recipe for", iWantThisManyCups, "hot chocolates")
print("-------------------------------------------")
print("Cups of milk:", cupsOfMilk)
print("Vanilla beans:", vanillaBeans)
print("Cinnamon sticks:", cinnamonSticks)
print("Ounces of chocolate:", ouncesOfChocolate)
print()
```

3.5 Exercises, Sample Code, Videos, And Addendums

Go to www.rdb3.com/python/3 for extended materials pertaining to this chapter.

Chapter 4. Doing The Math: Modules

Some problems are too difficult to solve with math operations only – for example, simple amortization. If you deposit $100 each month for 10 years, earning 7.5% interest per year compounded monthly, how much would you have at the end of those 10 years? Here's the formula for this (yikes!):

$$S = D\left(\frac{(1+p)^T - 1}{p}\right)$$

D is the deposit amount of $100 per month, S is the sum at the end of 10 years, p is the *monthly* interest rate (0.075 / 12), and T is the number of months in 10 years (10 * 12). All of this we can do with simple math operations, except for the part about raising something to the power of T. Actually, we could write 120 identical multiplication expressions, but there's got to be a better way! To solve this, we use the built-in math "module"! It contains useful expressions, like raise to a power, find the square root, trig, and exponentials. For example, to raise "x" to the power of "y", use this expression: `math.pow(x, y)`. `x` and `y` can be any numeric type.

Programmers refer to `math.pow(x, y)` as a "function call". Function names follow the same naming rules as variables, which involve the concept of "identifiers". Since identifiers identify both variables and functions, it makes it difficult to tell whether an identifier refers to a variable or a function. But there is an easy way to tell the difference – function calls always have *parentheses*. `len(s)` which we saw in the previous chapter, is a function call.

Here are some handy math functions that work with floating point values and variables:

math operation	in Python
square root	`math.sqrt(x)`
sine	`math.sin(x)`
cosine	`math.cos(x)`
raise "e" to a power	`math.exp(x)`
raise "x" to the power "y"	`math.pow(x, y)`

But note that in order to use the module of math functions in Python you need to have an `import math` statement before any of its functions get used – `import` statements are usually placed near the top of the source file.

"Modules" add functionality to a computer language – they add features that are not part of the base language. Think of them as expansion modules, like you might buy for a board game like "Settlers of Catan, Traders and Barbarians Expansion", or for a computer game like the "Halo 4 Multiplayer Map Pack". A feature to raise a number to a power is actually *not* part of the base Python computer language – it's in the "math" expansion module.

So here's the amortization calculation for an *annual* interest rate of 7.5% – make sure you understand the conversion of annual interest rate as a percent to monthly interest rate in decimal:

Example: Amortization Calculation [mort.py]

```
import math

# assignment upon declaration (see 3.2.3)
D = 100 # $ deposited per month
p = 0.075 / 12 # monthly rate
T = 10 * 12 # number of months

#the pow function call (new)
S = D * ((math.pow(1 + p, T) - 1) / p)

#the output
print(S)
```

Of course, there is an infinite number of ways to write the above code, including the choice of variable names and the use of one complex expression versus using several simpler expressions. Actually the variable names do not even conform to the convention of starting with lowercase letters. This deviation from convention was done to match the variables in the original equation, and this is an acceptable practice.

Also, note the use of `#` symbol in the above example. These denote "comments" – programmer's notes that are included in code but are ignored by Python. They are used throughout the rest of this book to refer back to other parts of the book where certain code structures were first introduced.

4.1 Formatting Output

Computer calculations are accurate. They are so accurate that computers feel they have to show all the digits behind the decimal. Consider `10 / 3` – the result is 3.33333333333333.... The computer likes to show all the 3's that it has, up to Python's default limit of 15 or so total digits. It may even throw in an extra, unexpected digit at the end! But you can force the computer to round off numbers and show them with a desired number of digits after the decimal.

You might expect that rounding actually changes the value stored in a variable, like from 3.333333 to 3.33. But it doesn't. The number is the number, and that's it! What's done instead is to get a *text* version of the number, made to look how you want it to look. Like this:

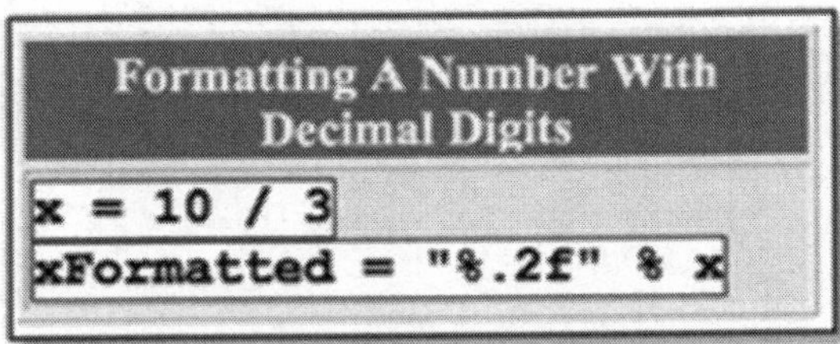

Formatting A Number With Decimal Digits

```
x = 10 / 3
xFormatted = "%.2f" % x
```

The new variable `xFormatted` stores a formatted *text* version of `x`, showing two decimal digits – that's what the `2` is there for. The number stored in `x` is unaffected – it's still 3 with all those 3's after its decimal point.

Here's the amortization calculation, with *formatted output*. Normally we do not apply rounding to *echoes* of input values – *echo* means to send an *input* value to output.

Complete Example: Amortization Calculation [`mort2.py`]

```
import math

# input values
years = 10 #number of years making monthly deposits
D = 100 #dollars deposited per month

# output (calculated) values
p = 0.075 / 12 # monthly rate
T = years * 12 # number of months
S = D * ((math.pow(1 + p, T) - 1) / p)

# echoing input values, not rounded
print("In", years, "years, $", end = "")
print(D, "deposited per month will grow to $", end = "")

# rounded output (see 4.1)
SFormatted = "%.2f" % S
print(SFormatted, ".", sep = "")
```

Note that a new variable was introduced: `years`. It is used in the calculation of `T`, but the real reason that it is specified separately is that it is included in the output statement. An alternative is to simply repeat the `10` in the output statement, but then the number would appear twice, and that is *not good programming practice*! What if you wanted to change the program for 8 years instead of 10? You'd have to find it and change it twice, which invites errors of typing and of omission.

Also note that there are two other formatting elements included in this example: `end` and `sep`. Normally each `print` statement outputs to its own new line. But in the program above, multiple `print` statements are used to build one output line. By putting `end = ""` at the end of the `print` statement, the next print statements begins where the last one left off. And have you noticed how the values placed in `print` statements with comma-separation always appear with a single space to separate them? We don't want a space before the period that ends the output. By putting `sep = ""` at the end of that `print` statement, there is no "`sep`aration" between output values.

There are many ways to have constructed the output sequence. The main reason for doing it the way it is done above is to fit the program listing on a page nicely, but it also shows the variety of ways that expressions can be combined.

Copy, save, and run this example. The result should be "In 10 years, $100 deposited per month will grow to $17793.03.". To put this into perspective, putting $100 per month into a piggy bank for 10 years would amount to $12,000, because there is zero interest in piggy banks.

4.1.1 Code Blocks

Usually it takes more that a single statement to do one thing in a program. For example, the rounded output section at the end of the Python sample program **mort2.py** requires 2 statements to complete. Similarly in written language it can take several sentences to complete a thought. In written English we use paragraphs to group related sentences together to form a thought. In programming we use *code blocks.*

Code blocks are written in programs purely for organizational purposes. Their use, correct or otherwise, has no impact on a program's operation.

Code blocks usually contain a comment line that explains the purpose of the code block, so that a reader of the program does not have to read all the statements in the code block in order to figure out what it does. Short code blocks do not always need a comment line, if they are easy to read and understand. To make code blocks easier to spot in a long program, skipped lines usually separate them. Here is what the output code block looks like with a comment line:

A Code Block With A Comment Line

```
# echo input and calculated values
print("In", years, "years, $", end = "")
print(D, "deposited per month will grow to $", end = "")
SFormatted = "%.2f" % S
print(SFormatted, ".", sep = "")
```

Code blocks with comment labels are used throughout the remainder of this book.

4.2 More Handy Modules And Functions

Besides modules for math and formatting, most computer languages have many additional modules with functions that perform complex operations that would be difficult for us to duplicate with the simple math operations supported by the language. Here are some of them, from the Python "string" and "math" modules:

Some More Handy Python Functions		
Function call	Explanation	Module
`x.upper()`	uppercase version of x, where x stores text	string
`x.lower()`	lowercase version of x, where x stores text	string
`math.fabs(x)`	absolute value of x, where x stores a number	`math`

It's important to remember that these function calls do *not* change the value of **`x`**. They simply *resolve* to that version of **`x`** for use in whatever statement contains the expression.

4.2.1 Conversion Statements

The Python function calls in the above table are all *expressions.* They are not stand-alone *statements* – it's important to understand the difference! They resolve to *new* values – they do not modify the original value stored in the variable **`x`**. In order to change a stored value, you need to use an expression in an assignment statement, as in these examples:

Some Handy Python Conversion Statements	
Statement	Explanation
`x = x.upper()`	replaces the text stored in x with its uppercase version; no effect if x's text contains no lowercase characters, a-z
`x = x.lower()`	replaces the text stored in x with its lowercase version; no effect if x's text contains no uppercase characters, A-Z
`x = math.fabs(x)`	replaces the number stored in x with its absolute value; no effect if x's value already non-negative

4.2.2 When To Use `import` Statements

Note that all the module function calls in this chapter have two words connected with a dot, and a pair of parentheses – sometimes empty, sometimes not. When the first word before the dot is a variable's name, there's no need for an import, because the word after the dot is already defined for the variable.

But for functions like the math functions, where the first word is a module name, you need to import that module so Python knows what you're talking about, since that word matches none of your variables. What this amounts to is that you need to import the "math" module, but not the "string" module.

4.3 Exercises, Sample Code, Videos, And Addendums

Go to www.rdb3.com/python/4 for extended materials pertaining to this chapter.

Chapter 5. Interactive Programs: Console I/O

Input can be gathered from a variety of sources. In chapters 3 and 4 we specified input values directly in the program source code. That worked fine, but if we wanted to use different input, such as changing the number of years in the amortization calculation, the program had to be edited. That is certainly not the kind of program that you could distribute for non-programmers to use!

It would be nice if the program could *prompt* (or ask) the user to type input values on the keyboard, and transfer those values into the variables in the program. Then we could develop the program only once, and it could be applied to a virtually unlimited range of input values.

This is what *interactive* programs do. They are designed for a certain amount of interaction to take place between the user and the program. This interaction transfers data values into variables, *after* the program has been written, while it is being run!

5.1 Capturing Values From The Keyboard

Capturing input from the keyboard involves three things in a Python code block:

3 Things You Need For Keyboard Input
1. A prompt to tell the user to type something and press ENTER. 2. A variable to store the value to be entered. 3. A Python `input` statement.

Here is a simple example:

Simple Example Of Console I/O [yourAge.py]

```
# code block to read a whole number from the keyboard
print("What is your age? ", end = "")
age = int(input())

# code block to echo the age of the user
print("Your age is", age)
```

This next sample program includes code blocks for reading text *and numbers*. Unlike the previous example, there are no output statements to echo the entered values to the console screen:

Transferring Values From The Keyboard [itsAboutYou.py]

```
# code block to read a whole number from the keyboard
print("What is your age? ", end = "")
age = int(input()) # store as a whole number

# code block to read a floating point number from the keyboard
print("What is your grade point average? ", end = "")
gpa = float(input()) # store as a floating point number

# code block to read text from the keyboard
print("What is your name? ", end = "")
name = input() # store as text (Python's default)

# code block to read a single character from the keyboard
print("What is your gender? [M/F]: ", end = "")
gender = input()[0] # store as a single character
```

There are four separate examples of keyboard input in the above code blocks – one for a whole number, one for a floating point number, and two for text. They are entirely independent of each other, and can be used in any combination to match the needs of your program. Each has (1) a user prompt, (2) a variable, (3) and the `input` function. As explained more fully below, prompts alert the user that the computer is waiting for something to be typed on the keyboard and the ENTER key pressed. Note that the prompts are enclosed in double-quote marks. If you want to have a double-quote mark as part of a prompt, you can use single-quote marks to contain the prompt text. Prompts are not required, but it's hard for a user to know what to do without them. It would be like staring at someone and waiting for them to answer, without you having asked a question!

Use these code blocks to add keyboard input to your programs by copying and adapting the sample code! (To adapt the code, change the variable names and prompts to suit your program.)

5.2 Prompts

The statements with `input` in them cause the program to pause and wait for the user to press the ENTER key before continuing. Program execution actually suspends there, waiting for the ENTER key to be pressed. Anything that is typed before the ENTER key gets pressed is then captured by the program, and can be stored in a variable. If nothing gets typed before pressing ENTER, there's no second chance – a blank, zero-length entry gets made, possibly resulting in an "invalid" input error that crashes and terminates the program!

On the computer screen, the only evidence of the `input` statement is a flashing symbol – usually a horizontal line in Windows or a box on a Mac. This is not very much of a clue for the user to know that something is supposed to be typed now, followed by the ENTER key. So we usually include instructions for the user in a prompt.

The following shows how a program would work without, and with a prompt.

With No Prompt:	With A Same-Line Prompt:	With A Previous-Line Prompt:

`name = input()`
_
	`print("Enter name: ", end = "")`
	`name = input()`
	Enter name: _
		`print("Enter name:")`
		`name = input()`
		Enter name:
		_

There are two ways to place the prompt: either on the same line where the user input is to be typed, or on the previous line. Both ways are shown above, but the same-line prompt is used in most of the example programs in this book. Note that the same-line prompt includes a separating space at the end of the prompt message (after the colon): `"Enter name: "` and an `end = ""` to prevent skipping to the next line. But the previous-line prompt does not have that space: `"Enter name:"`. Also, it is common to include possible responses in the prompt, enclosed in square brackets and separated by commas or slashes, like this: `"What is your gender? [M/F]: "`, as a guide to the user.

Unless you have a very good reason to do otherwise, *always* have a prompt for *each* user-entered value. Every time you expect the user to type something and press ENTER, or just to press ENTER after a pause, do this: include a prompt so that the user knows to do something. And if you can include some user guidance, such as possible responses or an example response, do so.

5.2.1 Simple Same-Line Prompts In Python

Since a same-line prompt with simple, short user instructions is the most common form of input, Python programmers usually use a feature of `input` that allows prompt text to be included inside its parentheses, thus avoiding the separate `print` statement. Here are some examples – note the space at the end of each prompt's text to separate the prompt from the user's response:

Using Same-Line Prompts – A Shortcut [sameLinePrompts.py]

```
age = int(input("What is your age? ")) # whole number

gpa = float(input("What is your grade point average? ")) # floating point number

name = input("What is your name? ") # text

gender = input("What is your gender? [M/F]: ")[0] # single character
```

5.3 Interrupting An Interactive Program

Sometimes in the process of writing and testing a program that has console input, it may be convenient to terminate (that is, end or exit) a program early. For example, if the input involves a series of prompts, you may notice incorrect spelling in the first prompt. In order to stop right away and fix it, rather than continue on through the remaining prompts and normal termination of the program, you can type CTRL-C to make the program stop. On a PC, hold down the *CTRL* (or *control*) key, press the letter C key, and then release both. On a Mac, it's the *control* key and the C key.

5.4 Exercises, Sample Code, Videos, And Addendums

Go to www.rdb3.com/python/5 for extended materials pertaining to this chapter.

PART 2 Programming Logic

Chapter 9. Counting On Your Fingers: Bits And Bytes
9.1 Computer Memory: Vast Arrays Of On/Off Switches
9.2 Floating Point Numbers
9.3 Representing Characters
9.4 The True/False, Yes/No, On/Off, Up/Down, Left/Right Data Type
9.5 Literal Values
9.6 Type Conversion
9.7 Exercises, Sample Code, Videos, And Addendums

Chapter 10. Interactive Programs: File I/O
10.1 Text File Input
10.2 Text File Output
10.3 Exercises, Sample Code, Videos, And Addendums

Chapter 6. Simple Logic: Basic Branching/Looping

As shown in chapter 1, branching and looping are ways to make programs more interesting and useful by allowing them to skip and jump around among statements, rather than follow a strict sequence from top to bottom with no options. The decision points in programs where the flow of the program can either continue in a sequence or skip to somewhere else involves "logic" – something like, "if this condition exists, then do something – otherwise, skip over that something".

6.1 The If-Statement

In both of the following examples, the *indented* output statement gets executed *only* if the user's guess is correct. This is the basic "if-statement" for use in branching – it allows branching *over* the indented statement.

Using Branching Logic [oneToTen.py]

```
# read a score from the keyboard (see 5.1 and 5.2.1)
print("I am thinking of a number between 1-10")
usersGuess = int(input("Try to guess the number [1-10]: "))

# see if the guess is right
if usersGuess == 7:
  print("You guessed it!")
```

More Branching Logic [Rumpelstiltskin.py]

```
# read text from the keyboard (see 5.2.1)
usersGuess = input("Try to guess my name: ")

# see if the guess is right
if usersGuess == "Rumpelstiltskin":
  print("Argh!!!")
print("GOODBYE")
```

These if-statements begin with the lowercase word `if`. After that, values and variables are compared to see if they are equal. If so, the next, *indented* line gets included, otherwise not. That odd-looking, two-character symbol is double-equals, `==`. It tells the program to compare based on equality.

Note that there is a colon at the end of the `if ...:` statements, unlike other Python statements. It means that if the comparison turns out to be true, then do what follows in the indented line(s) of code.

In the second program, GOODBYE gets sent to output no matter what – only one line, the indented one, belongs to the if-statement. Unlike other languages like C++ and Java, indenting *does* matter in Python!

6.2 Comparison Operators

Along with `==`, there are six commonly used "operators". An operator is something that uses the values and/or variables next to it and does something with them. The following table lists some operators that *compare* values and variables:

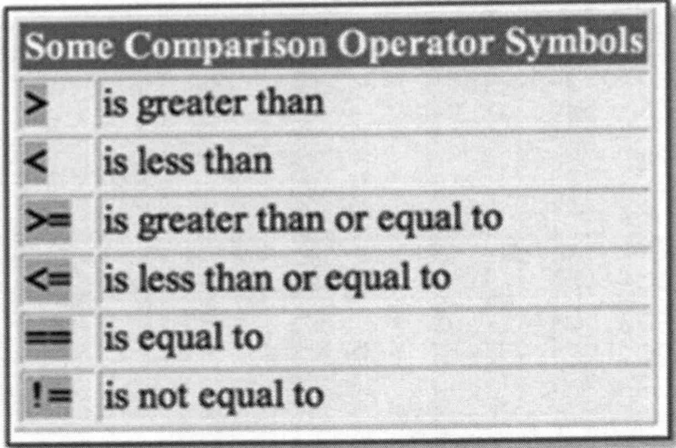

Some Comparison Operator Symbols	
>	is greater than
<	is less than
>=	is greater than or equal to
<=	is less than or equal to
==	is equal to
!=	is not equal to

The symbols for some of these operators consist of *two characters*. They should be typed without being separated by spaces. When an operator is typed with two numbers, variables, or expressions on either side of it, the result is a *simple logical expression*, like `number == 7`. There are single spaces separating the operator symbol from the two items it compares – these are not required, but are there for readability.

Here are some examples of simple logical expressions, which could be placed after the `if` and before the `:` of an if-statement:

Examples Of Logical Expressions, Using Comparison Operators	
`x < 10`	tests whether the *numeric* value stored in x is less than 10 (x must be an already-declared variable, containing either a whole number or floating point value.
`s == "Hello"`	tests whether the text stored in s is exactly equal to "Hello", with matching case (s must contain text).
`a != b`	tests whether a and b have different values (a and b must both contain numbers, or both contain text)
`gender == 'F'`	tests whether gender is uppercase F (gender must contain text)

It is important to remember that the test for equality has *two* back-to-back equal signs. You may recall that a single equal sign already means something: assignment of a value to a variable. So a different symbol is needed for the equality operator. It is not possible to have `x = 10` (with just one equal sign) in an if-statement, because Python sees it as an error.

6.2.1 This AND That

Sometimes it is convenient to test for a range of values, or test for more than one possible value of a variable. For that reason, most computer languages let you put multiple logical expressions together in such a way that they *all* have to be satisfied in order for the if-statement to evaluate to true. Here's an example: "if the test score is greater or equal to 80, *and* less than 90, then assign a grade of B." Here's an example: "if the score is 80-89, the student's grade is B."

```
the algorithm for and-logic:
read a score from the keyboard as a whole number
if the score is 80 or greater AND less than 90
    output "grade B"
```

Using And-Logic [gradeB.py]

```
# read a score from the keyboard (see 5.2.1)
score = int(input("What is your test score? [0-100]: "))

# see if score is in the B range
if score >= 80 and score < 90:
  print("Your grade is B")
```

The word that joins two (or more) simple logical expressions with "and-logic" is `and`, and the result is a "compound logical expression". Note that there is repetition in the if-statement – `score` is typed twice. There is no easy way to say "if the score is greater than or equal to 80 and less than 90" in Python. You should just say "if the score is greater than or equal to 80 *and* the score less than 90" instead.

It might not make any difference to you now, but the computer does not always need to evaluate all of the simple logical expressions when using and-logic. For example, if the score is 50, the "greater than or equal to 80" part is false, so there is no point in checking if "the score less than 90".

6.2.2 This OR That

It's also possible to combine multiple logical expressions such that *any one* has to be satisfied in order for the if-statement to evaluate to true. The following example shows how to use "or-logic": "if the grade is A, B, or C, the student passes the class":

the algorithm for or-logic:

```
read a grade from the keyboard as a single letter
if the grade is uppercase A, B, or C
    output "you pass"
```

Using Or-Logic [passingGrade.py]

```
# read a score from the keyboard (see 5.1)
grade = input("What is your grade? [A, B, C, D, or F]: ")
grade = grade[0] # read only the first character

# check for passing grade
if grade == 'A' or grade == 'B' or grade == 'C':
  print("You pass")
```

The word that joins two (or more) simple logical expressions with or-logic is `or`. Note that there is repetition in the statement – `grade` is typed three times. You do not say "if the grade is A or B or C" in code, using `or`. You say, "if the grade is A *or* the grade is B *or* the grade is C" instead.

Again, computers do not always need to evaluate all of the simple logical expressions in or-logic. For example, if the grade is A, the "grade is A" part is true, so there is no point in checking if the "grade is B" or if the "grade is C".

6.2.3 This AND That OR That OR Something Else

Be careful – it is possible to join simple logical expressions with `and`s and `or`s all in the same if-statement. But this is usually not a good idea, because the exact meaning of the logic can be confusing. It has to do with the order in which operations are evaluated, left to right. For example, don't do `score >= 0 and score < 80 or score >= 90 and score <= 100` to test for scores that are not B. But you can force the order of evaluation of the logical expressions using parentheses like this: `(score >= 0 and score < 80) or (score >= 90 and score <= 100)`! Inside an if-statement, it would look like this:

```
if (score >= 0 and score < 80)

or (score >= 90 and score <= 100):
```

.

Also note that the variable that appears multiple times in complex logical expressions does not have to be the same variable in each of the simple logical expressions. You can do this, for example: `score > 86 and grade == 'B'` to test for a high B.

6.2.4 Handling "Case"

What if the prompt for grade tells the user to enter an uppercase letter grade, but the user types a lowercase letter instead? After all, the letters are shown in uppercase on console keyboard keys! Rather than not recognize "a" as "A", you can do one of two things: check for either case, or *temporarily* convert case before checking the value. For example:

`grade == 'A' or grade == 'a'` or `grade.upper() == 'A'`

6.3 True/False If-Statements

Often it is convenient to use logic to switch between two possible code blocks – one if a comparison is true, and another if it's false. This is possible using two different if-statements with opposite comparison expressions, but an easier way is to append an `else:` clause to the end of the if-statement, thereby applying "if-else logic". Here's an example:

```
the algorithm for if-else logic:
read a grade from the keyboard as a single letter
if the grade is uppercase A, B, or C
    output "you pass"
otherwise
    output "you don't pass"
```

Using If-Else Logic [passNoPass.py]

```
# read a score from the keyboard (see 5.2.1)
grade = input("What is your grade? [A, B, C, D, or F]: ")[0]

# check for passing grade
if grade == 'A' or grade == 'B' or grade == 'C':
  print("You pass")
else:
  print("You do not pass")
```

The `else:` is followed by another output statement to be used in case the if-statement's condition evaluates to false. Note that `else:` cannot be used in Python unless it follows an if-statement at the same level of indent.

6.4 Indented Code Blocks

Up to now, the if-statements we've considered have all been associated with single output statements. That is, if the if-statement's condition evaluates to true, then execute the following indented statement. But what if you want to execute more than one statement?

To include multiple lines, *indent them all exactly the same*. An equal number of spaces of indenting is what groups adjacent Python statements together in a single "code block". Parentheses and square brackets group things together on the same line. Indenting groups things on multiple lines.

When you indent a code block right below an if-statement (or below `else:` indent each line with the same number of spaces – this book recommends 2 spaces. Here's an example:

The 2-Space Indented Code Block

```
if score >= 90:
  print("Your grade is A")
  numberOfAs = numberOfAs + 1
```

6.5 The While-True Loop

The if-statement implements branching; the *while-true loop* implements looping back. Loops consist of statements that are to be repeated by looping from *after* the last statement, back up to *before* the first. Each pass through a loop is called a "cycle".

A while-true loop begins with the `while True:` statement followed by an indented code block – just like the ones used with if-statements and introduced earlier in this chapter. Here's an example:

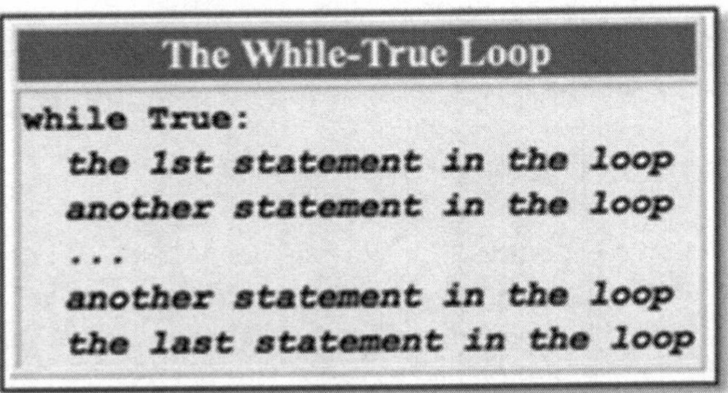

Note that there is colon at the end of the `while True:` statement – same as `if ...:`.

Here is a modification to **passingGrade.py** program from earlier in this chapter, which now allows an unlimited number of repeats in what programmers call an "infinite loop".

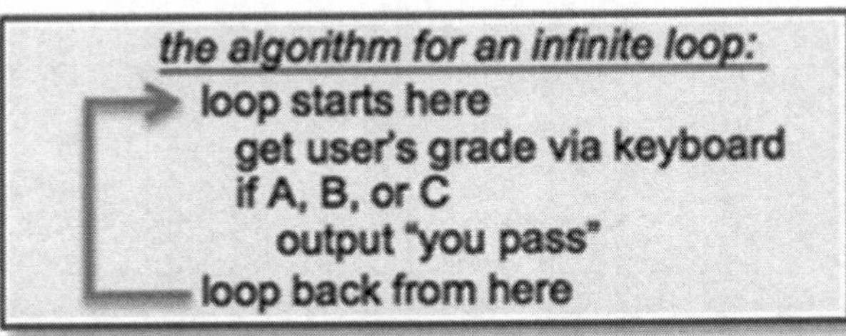

An Infinite Loop [passingGradeL.py]

```
while True:

  # read a score from the keyboard (see 5.2.1)
  grade = input("What is your grade? [A, B, C, D, or F]: ")[0]

  # check for passing grade
  if grade == 'A' or grade == 'B' or grade == 'C':
    print("You pass")
```

This loops over and over, actually never ending! The way out of this loop is to press CTRL-C (or control-C) instead of typing a grade when prompted. There really should be a prompt that tells the user to "Use CTRL-C to quit...". But relying on CTRL-C to end a program is really not good programming practice. We come up with a better way in the next section.

Note however that the only differences between the above program and its predecessor are (1) insertion of the looping code, and (2) indenting of the code block. So looping is *very easy* to implement in Python code.

6.5.1 Infinite Loops

As already mentioned, what we created in the above example is called an infinite loop, because it repeats over and over, to infinity. There is no way to end the program normally. CTRL-C (or control-C) ends it, but it ends the *program*, not just the loop. If there were any more code after the loop to be processed, it would be skipped upon CTRL-C (or control-C).

You don't want your program to get stuck in an infinite loop. You need to design a way out of the loop that does not kill the program, and that's where the "if-break" statement comes in.

6.6 The While-True-If-Break Loop

The purpose of *if-break* is to define a condition under which looping would discontinue, and sequential processing would pick up at the first statement *after* the loop's indented code block. For example, the user could enter a grade of X to indicate that the **passingGradeL.py** program should stop looping and skip to the end. Adding one or more if-break statements to a while-true loop gives you a while-true-if-break loop, with a way out of the loop that does not kill the program. Here's an example:

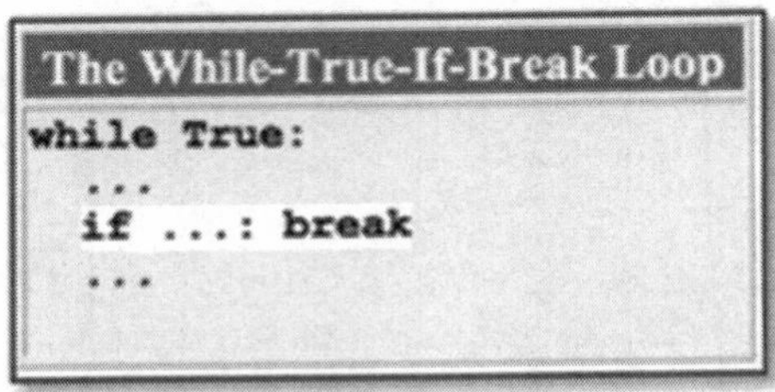

For example, after reading the grade in the above example, you could add the statement `if grade == 'X': break`. Of course, you need to let the user know about this feature, so the prompt may change to something like this: `"What is your grade? [A, B, C, D, F, or X to quit]: "`. It would look something like this:

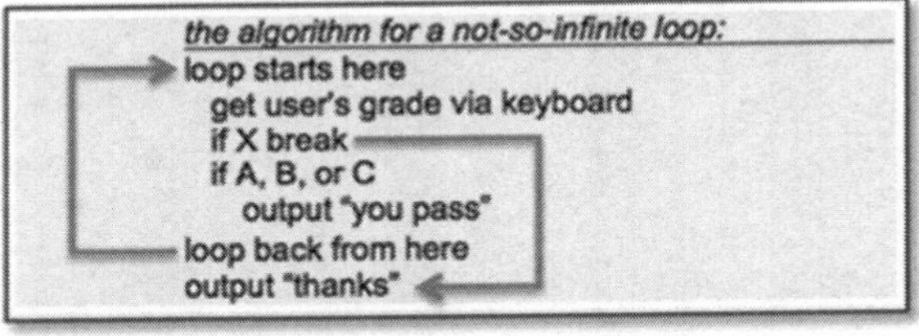

A Not-So-Infinite Loop [passingGradeIB.py]

```
while True:

  # read a score from the keyboard (see 5.2.1)
  grade = input("What is your grade? [A, B, C, D, F, or X to quit]: ")[0]

  if grade == 'X' or grade == 'x': break

  # check for passing grade
  if grade == 'A' or grade == 'B' or grade == 'C':
    print("You pass")
```

Note the minor enhancement added to this program – it accepts uppercase *or* lowercase X to end the loop. (This is what's known as a *sentinel* – it signifies the end of a process.) The program also sends a thank you note to output before the program ends.

6.7 Bringing It All Together: Programming With Logic

This section contains code examples using `if` and `while`. You can copy, save, and run them. You can modify them and see how they work. Make sure that you understand everything in each of these examples.

6.7.1 Another Infinite Loop

Here is another program with an infinite loop. Note that the prompt instructs the user to press CTRL-C to stop the program.

Another Infinite Loop [tempConvert.py]

```
while True:

   c = float(input("Enter temperature in Celsius [CTRL-C to exit]: "))
   f = 9 / 5 * c + 32
   f = "%.1f" % f # convert number to formatted text
   print("The temperature in degrees F is ", f) # see 3.4.1
```

The above example uses the ill-advised CTRL-C to exit the loop – see if you can think of a better way to end the program!

6.7.2 A Quiz Program

The following example shows a quiz with one math question (8+2=?). It demonstrates some formatting code, too, so that the prompts are aligned and not fully left justified at the edge of the screen.

```
the algorithm for a quiz program:
prompt the user with the quiz question for 8 + 2
read the user's answer from the keyboard
if the answer is 10
    output "correct"
otherwise
    output "incorrect"
```

A Quiz Program [quiz.py]

```
# read an int using a very lengthy prompt
print("\n\n\n")
print("       8")
print("      +2")
print("      --")
print("      ", end="")
answer = int(input()) # see 5.1

print("      ", end = "")
if answer == 10: # see 6.1
  print("Correct!")
else: # see 6.3
  print("Very good, but a better answer is 10")
```

Note the `print("\n\n\n")` statement in the quiz program. Each `\n` skips one line. It's called a "line break". Since there are 3 of them, and since the statement itself skips a line, four lines are skipped. This is done just to clear some space.

The output statements contain leading spaces inside the quote marks – this is to move the "8" and the "+2" over from the extreme left edge of the console window. The spaces are arranged so that the "2" in "+2" aligns under the "8" above it. Also note the statement that contains the two dashes (`--`) looks like the horizontal line you would draw if you were to write this math problem on a piece of paper.

6.7.3 Simple While-True-If-Break Loops

Here are some programs that use if-break to exit a loop.

A Simple Loop [thereYet.py]

```
while True:

  answer = input("Are we there yet [yes/no]? ")
  if answer == "yes": break # see 6.6

print("We're home!")
```

Another Simple Loop [crossTheRoad.py]

```
print("Approach the curb.")
while True:

  answer = input("Look both ways. Is it clear [Y/N]? ")[0]
  if answer == 'Y' or answer == 'y': break

print("It's safe to cross!")
```

In the sample above, note that we don't even check for the user to input "N". What's going on is this: "Y" is considered as yes – so is "y". *Anything else* is considered "no". To avoid confusion, it might be better to not accept answers other than "Y" or "N". That's what "validation loops" are for.

6.7.4 Validation Loops

Validation loops are used with console input to make sure the user types valid entries. These loops repeat until a valid value is received, and usually output a message after detecting invalid input and before doing another cycle of the loop. Here is code block that prompts for grades to be entered:

Without Validation

```
grade = input("What is your grade? [A, B, C, D, F, or X to quit]: ")[0]

# now do something with "grade"
...
```

With A Validation Loop

```
while True:

  grade = input("What is your grade? [A, B, C, D, F, or X to quit]: ")[0]

  if grade == 'A' or grade == 'B' or grade == 'C' \
     or grade == 'D' or grade == 'F' or grade.upper() == 'X': break

# now do something with "grade"
...
```

Let's study the above code, because it not only demonstrates a validation loop, but it demonstrates two new code features. The most important is that the variable `grade` be declared *inside* the validation loop, and it's still usable *after* the loop. Once a variable has been defined in a program like the ones we're writing here, it's defined until the program ends – at least until we get to subprograms. This is what's referred to as *scope*.

The Scope Of A Variable

```
if...:
  ...
  a = ...
  ..."a" is usable starting here...

...and here, after the indented code block
```

The other new feature is the backslash `\` -- it's for line continuation. It allows the programmer to force wrap long statements. The validation if-break statement is very lengthy because it has so many tests in it. It's okay to have very long lines in most computer languages, but it makes it hard to read. You could use line wrap in your text editor to see long lines, but it does not follow the indenting rules. So the solution is to split long statements onto separate lines. But do not split in the middle of a word or inside quoted text.

When splitting a statement to two or more lines, you don't actually have to indent the second and succeeding lines, but it's a good idea to do so for readability. In the above example, the normal indent of 2 spaces is used, just as it is with indented code blocks after if-statements.

As an alternative, the long if-break could have been separated into multiple if-breaks, like this:

```
if grade == 'A' or grade == 'B': break
if grade == 'C' or grade == 'D': break
if grade == 'F' or grade == 'X' or grade == 'x': break
```

Here's another example of a validation loop:

Another Validation Loop

```
while True:

  answer = input("Your answer [yes/no]: ")
  if answer == '': continue
  if answer == 'yes': break
  if answer == 'no': break
  print("Let's try this again...")

# resume here after "break"
```

Note the `continue` statement introduced above. This causes the loop to end the current cycle at that point and go automatically to the next cycle, thus avoiding the "Let's try this again..." prompt if a user just pressed ENTER without typing anything else. There's really no good reason for doing so, other than the opportunity this presents to show how `continue` works.

6.8 Classic Computer Science Solutions That Use Logic

Two classic problems are finding the lowest (or highest) from among a set of values, and sorting a set of value from lowest to highest (or the reverse). The solutions involve if-statements. They also involve techniques that will be covered in chapters 8 and 11, so while we cannot develop full solutions here, we can at least show the logical parts of the solutions.

6.8.1 Classic Min/Max Logic

A classic problem in computer science is finding the minimum and/or maximum values from among multiple values. For example, given a set of test scores, what are the highest and lowest scores? We still need to get through chapter 11 before we can fully deal with this problem. But now that we can apply logic in our programming, we can at least get a start on the solution. Here are some code blocks to show how this is done:

Finding The Maximum Or Minimum Value

```
# get values for 3 whole numbers
a = ...
b = ...
c = ...
```

```
# find the maximum whole number
maximum = a
if maximum < b: maximum = b
if maximum < c: maximum = c
```

```
# find the minimum whole number
minimum = a
if minimum > b: minimum = b
if minimum > c: minimum = c
```

You may not have come up with this logic on your own right away, because it is somewhat counter-intuitive. For example, note that there are variables for storing the minimum and maximum values, but they are set to the value of *the first number*! It's as if we know the answer in advance, and the answer is the first number – we'd have to be pretty lucky for this to work every time!

But the situation is that our if-statements can only compare 2 values at a time, and we have 3. So here's the approach: without looking at any of the numbers, *assume* that the first number is what we want. Then look at the second number, and if it is better, *we change our mind!* Then look at the third number, and if *it* is better, we change our mind, perhaps again. Get used to the idea, because that's a very common approach in programming – assume the answer, then look at alternatives and change your mind when necessary.

You can probably figure out how to extend this to 4 or more values – just add more if-statements.

6.8.2 Classic Sorting Logic

Another classic problem in computer science is reordering multiple values from lowest to highest (or the reverse). We need to get through chapter 11 before we can fully deal with this problem, but we can start here.

Sorting Values Lo-to-Hi

```
# get values for 3 numbers
a = ...
b = ...
c = ...

# move the lowest value to "a"
if a > b:
  a,b = b,a #swap a and b

if a > c:
  a,c = c,a # swap a and c

# move the next lowest value to "b"
if b > c:
  b,c = c,b # swap b and c

# ...the highest value is now in "c"
```

Wow – there's a lot of code here! But most of it is repetitious, and will get consolidated as we revisit this in future chapters. Note the statements to swap the contents of two variables.

6.9 Exercises, Sample Code, Videos, And Addendums

Go to www.rdb3.com/python/6 for extended materials pertaining to this chapter

Chapter 7. More Than One Way: Advanced Branching/Looping

In part 1 of this book we learned to write Python statements to be processed in sequential order, top to bottom. Then in the previous chapter, we learned how statements and code blocks could be skipped over (using if-statements) or repeated (using while-true loops). In this chapter we'll learn other ways to implement branching and looping besides if-statements, if-else, while-true, and if-break. They don't really *add* anything to what we can already do, but they offer us *more concise ways* to write code under certain conditions.

7.1 Multiple Choice If-Statements

Adding `else:` after an if-statement, as explained in the previous chapter, simplifies writing code for "true-false" comparisons. The same could be accomplished with *two* separate if-statements, but it's much easier using *one* if-statement with an `else:`

True-False Logic WITHOUT Else

```
if grade == 'A' or grade == 'B' or grade == 'C':
  print("You pass")
if grade != 'A' and grade != 'B' and grade != 'C':
  print("You do not pass")
```

True-False Logic WITH Else – Much Easier!

```
if grade == 'A' or grade == 'B' or grade == 'C':
  print("You pass")
else:
  print("You do not pass")
```

Similarly, it's even more complicated to program "multiple choice" comparisons using lots of separate if-statements, so the Python language does offer another, more direct way, called `elif` -- an abbreviation meaning "else if".

Using "else-if" logic, if-statements can have zero, one, two, or more `elif`s to test for multiple choices. Once an `if` or `elif` is found to be true, no further checking of any remaining `elif`s happens. There can be an `else:` at the end, or not, but it *must* come after any `elif`s. Each `elif` has its own indented statement or code block.

Here's an example:

the algorithm for else-if logic:
get user's grade via keyboard
if A, output "excellent"
otherwise if B, output "good"
otherwise if C, output "average"
otherwise if D or F, output "see ya..."
otherwise, output "invalid"

Using Else-If Logic [grades.py]

```
# read a grade from the keyboard (see 5.2.1)
grade = input("What is your grade? [A, B, C, D, or F]: ")[0]

# check for passing grade
if grade == 'A':
  print("Excellent")
elif grade == 'B':
  print("Good")
elif grade == 'C':
  print("Average")
elif grade == 'D' or grade == 'F':
  print("See you next year")
else:
  print("Invalid:", grade)
```

Another example shows how to compare two numbers, in order to find which is greater – or if they are the same. It uses else-if logic, and the `else:` is reached when neither number is greater than the other – that is, they are the same. There's no need to check with `==` because there's nothing else it could be!

```
the algorithm for comparing two numbers:
read the 1st number from the keyboard
read the 2nd number from the keyboard
if the 1st number is smaller than the 2nd
   output that it is so
otherwise if the 2nd number is smaller than the 1st
   output that it is so
otherwise
   output that the numbers are the same
```

Comparing Numbers With Else-If [compare2Numbers.py]

```
a = int(input("Enter the 1st number: "))
b = int(input("Enter the 2nd number: "))

if a < b:
  print(a, "is less than", b)
elif b < a:
  print(b, "is less than", a)
else:
  print(a, "is the same as", b)
```

If you're a C++ or Java programmer and you're wondering where is the *switch-statement*, Python does not have one!

7.2 Event-Controlled vs Count-Controlled Loops

There are two basic loop types: "event-controlled" and "count-controlled". The difference is a conceptual one, having to do with knowing *in advance* the number of cycles the loop will execute. In event-controlled loops, cycles continue until certain conditions are met that allow an if-break to exit the loop. When such conditions are met, that's an "event". The number of cycles that will be executed before the event occurs cannot be determined ahead of time. Every loop example in the previous chapter was event-controlled.

The types of event that can cause the end of an event-controlled loop include (1) user enters “quit” in response to a prompt, (2) a valid input value is entered, (3) the end of a file is reached while reading a file, as we’ll study in chapter 10, or (4) satisfying any other logical condition that should make the loop end.

By contrast, a count-controlled loop executes a *predetermined* number of cycles. So a loop that prints your name repeatedly until the user tells it to stop is *event-controlled.* And a loop to output your name exactly 10 times is *count-controlled.*

If the number of cycles of a loop is known ahead of time, use a *count-controlled loop.* It’s similar to an event-controlled loop, but the “event” is reaching the predetermined number of cycles. Count-controlled loops use a “counter” variable to keep track of the number of cycles, and it is the value of this “counter” that is compared in an “if-break“.

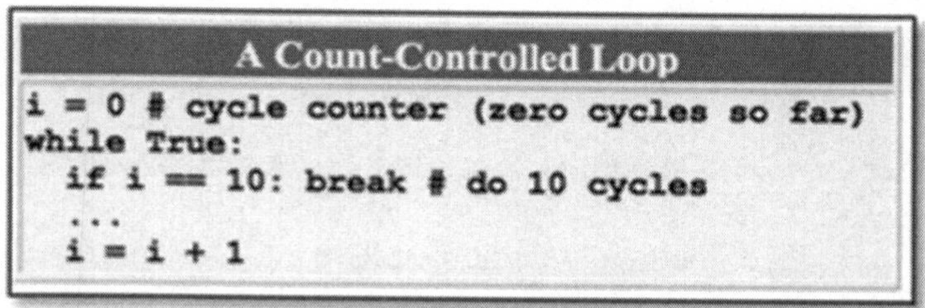
A Count-Controlled Loop

```
i = 0 # cycle counter (zero cycles so far)
while True:
  if i == 10: break # do 10 cycles
  ...
  i = i + 1
```

The counter in count-controlled loops is traditionally declared as `i`. The last statement in the loop “increments” `i` – that is, it adds one to it. But the logic to control this loop is all over the place – before the loops starts, at the top of the loop’s indented code block, and at the bottom of the code block. The purpose of this chapter is to introduce other ways to do such loops in more concise ways.

Actually the counter can be incremented anywhere else in the loop, and it can still work the same. But it’s better to perform the incrementing at the *end* of the loop for reasons that will become clearer as we go forward.

7.2.1 The While-Condition Loop

In the next example, the previous count-controlled loop is simplified a little bit by putting something other than `True` after `while`:

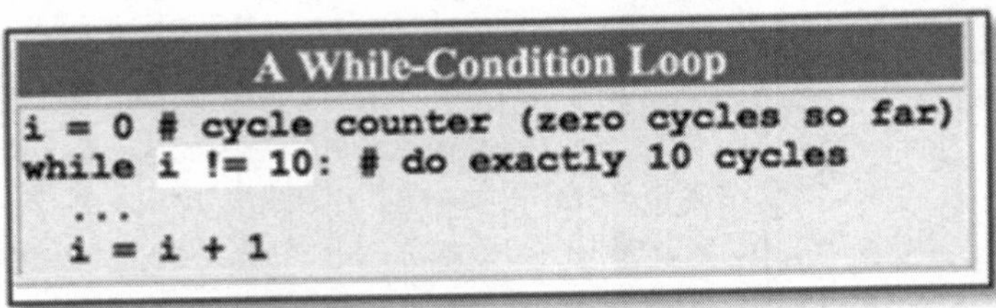

A While-Condition Loop

```
i = 0 # cycle counter (zero cycles so far)
while i != 10: # do exactly 10 cycles
  ...
  i = i + 1
```

The while-condition statement combines the while-true and if-break into *one* statement. Instead of breaking when the counter reaches 10, we continue the loop as long as the counter is *not* 10. The if-break's condition got moved to after the `while`, but its logic had to be *reversed*! Break if equal, keep going while *not* equal.

While-condition can be used for both event-controlled and count-controlled loops. Remember – count-controlled loops are really just event-controlled loops where the "event" is the counter reaching its limit.

Here's the rule for when you can use while-condition instead of while-true-if-break: if there's an if-break statement as the *first statement* inside the loop's indented code block, you can use while-condition instead. You don't have to, but you can.

Here is a full example of a *count-controlled loop* using while-condition. It tracks the height that a dropped ball bounces, by cutting the height by 50% with each successive bounce. It tracks this for exactly 10 bounces, starting from a height of 40 (inches).

A Simple Count-Controlled Loop [bounce.py]

```
height = 40

i = 0 # declare and initialize a loop counter
while i != 10:
  height = height / 2
  print("location is now:", height, " inches")
  i = i + 1
```

The last statement in this count-controlled loop *increments* the counter, `i`. Since incrementing `i` is done so often in programming, Python has a shorthand way to write `i = i + 1` – it's `i += 1`. And yes, there's an `i -= 1` too, that subtracts 1 from `i`. In fact, any number other that `1` can also be used, too.

If you're a C++ or Java programmer, and you're wondering where is the *do-while* loop, there is none in Python! There's no `++` or `--` either.

7.3 Introducing The For-Loop

Count-controlled loops have three control steps that are each done separately but are all required in order for the loop to work right. So like most languages, Python provides a variation called the "for-loop", which combines all three into one statement. Here's an adaptation of **bounce.py** from above, using a for-loop:

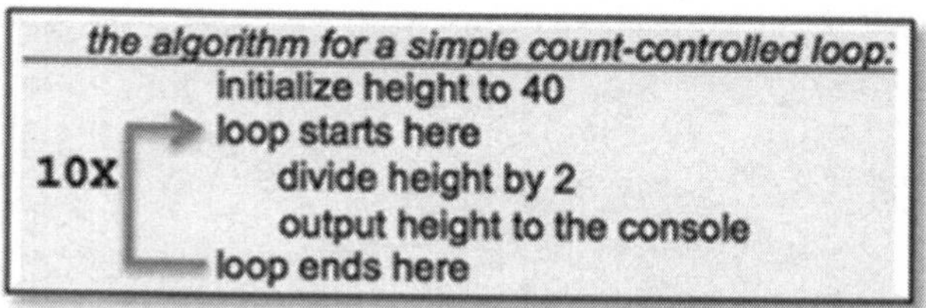

the algorithm for a simple count-controlled loop:
initialize height to 40
loop starts here
10X
divide height by 2
output height to the console
loop ends here

A Simple Count-Controlled Loop [bounce2.py]

```
height = 40

for i in range(10):
  height = height / 2
  print("location is now:", height, " inches")
```

The `for` statement has two distinct parts to it. The first part declares an internal counter `i` for the loop to use in counting its cycles. The second part specifies the number of cycles to execute.

7.3.1 Variable For-Loop Cycle Limit

In the for-loops presented above, the limit is expressed as a number – 10. That is, the loop will run for exactly 10 cycles. But the limit can also be expressed as a whole number *variable*. In the next example, the user specifies via the keyboard how many numbers to send to output, starting with one:

Counting From Zero [countFromZero.py]

```
n = int(input("How many numbers to output? "))

number = 1 # start with this number
for i in range(n):
  print(number, end=" ") # for separation
  number += 1 # go to the next number

print() # skip to the next line
```

output: 1 2 3 4 5 6 ...

7.3.2 Counting Backwards

Here's an example that sends a numeric sequence of 16 numbers to output, *backwards* from 99:

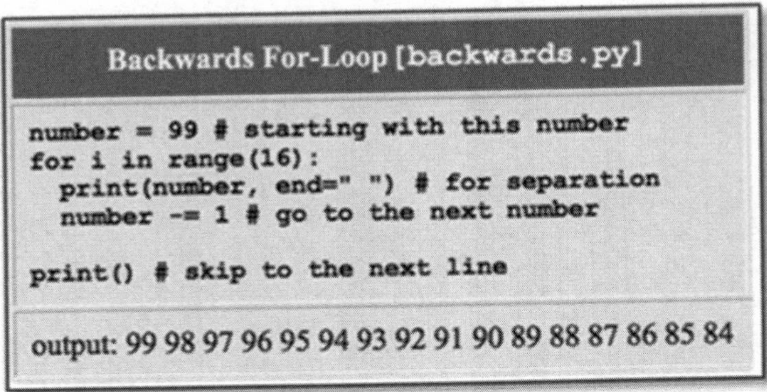

Backwards For-Loop [backwards.py]

```
number = 99 # starting with this number
for i in range(16):
  print(number, end=" ") # for separation
  number -= 1 # go to the next number

print() # skip to the next line
```

output: 99 98 97 96 95 94 93 92 91 90 89 88 87 86 85 84

7.3.3 Classic Min/Max Loop

As it was presented in the previous chapter, a classic min/max problem is finding the largest and smallest among three values. In this variation we find the largest and smallest among an *unlimited* number of values, using an event-controlled loop. The loop is controlled using the "sentinel method" – when the user enters a certain value outside of the expected range of values, it is a signal to exit the loop. As in the example from the previous chapter, we use test scores whose values are expected to be in the range of 0 to 100. Here are some code blocks that show how this is done:

Finding The Maximum Or Minimum Value Using Loops

```
# find the maximum score
sentinel = -999 # an unexpected score value
maximum = sentinel # signifies that maximum is not yet set

while True:
  print("Enter a score [", sentinel, "to exit]: ")
  aScore = int(input()) # see 5.1
  if aScore == sentinel: break # that's the signal to exit this loop
  if maximum == sentinel or maximum < aScore: maximum = aScore
```

```
# find the minimum score
sentinel = -999 # an unexpected score value
minimum = sentinel # signifies that maximum is not yet set

while True:
  print("Enter a score [", sentinel, "to exit]: ")
  aScore = int(input()) # see 5.1
  if aScore == sentinel: break # that's the signal to exit this loop
  if minimum == sentinel or minimum > aScore: minimum = aScore
```

```
# find the maximum and minimum scores
sentinel = -999 # an unexpected score value
maximum  = sentinel # signifies that maximum is not yet set
minimum = sentinel # signifies that maximum is not yet set

while True:
  print("Enter a score [", sentinel, "to exit]: ")
  aScore = int(input()) # see 5.1
  if aScore == sentinel: break # that's the signal to exit this loop
  if maximum == sentinel or maximum < aScore: maximum = aScore
  if minimum == sentinel or minimum > aScore: minimum = aScore
```

The `if aScore == sentinel: break` statement is easy to understand – it exits the loop if the sentinel value gets entered. But what about `if maximum == sentinel ...`? That's there so that the maximum and/or minimum get set to the first-entered value no matter what it is. Remember that the first-entered value will necessarily be the maximum *and* the minimum until something else comes along to replace it.

Try this modification: you can avoid the issue of a sentinel if you first prompt the user for the number of scores to be entered. But you still have to figure out how to initialize `maximum` and `minimum`. An old trick is to initialize `maximum` to a very large negative number, so that no matter what the first entry is, it will be larger. Likewise, initialize `minimum` to a very large positive number, so that no matter what the first entry is, it will be smaller.

Here is another feature of the above code blocks that you should notice and learn by the example it provides. Note that `sentinel` is created to store `-999`, and note that the value `-999` therefore only has to appear once. It is good programming practice to write a value only once, so that if you change it, you only have to do so in one place. You'll see that this requires the "Enter a score" prompt to be a bit more complicated than usual, to include `sentinel`.

7.4 Nested Loops

"Nesting" is when there is a loop *inside* the indented code block of another loop. In each cycle of the outer-most loop, *all* cycles if the innermost loop are run. The concept of nesting is not just for for-loops – it's for loops in general, both count-controlled and event-controlled. But the examples that follow are all nested for-loops. Nested count-controlled loops need *two* loop counters – one to remember how many times we've been through the "outer loop" while another counts the cycles of the "inner loop".

A classic programming puzzle is to use nested loops to create two-dimensional patterns in rows and columns of the output. For example, here is a program that reads a number for the keyboard, and outputs that many rows of stars. The first row contains one star, and each succeeding row contains one additional star. Note that this uses a variable `n` for the cycle limit.

Right-Triangle Pattern [rightTriangle.py]

```
n = int(input("How many rows to output? "))

for i in range(n): # outer loop
  for j in range(i + 1): # inner loop
    print("*", end="")
  print()
```

Look at the j-loop. It cycles `i + 1` times. We've ignored counter variables up to now, but now it's time to make use of them. Counters start at 0, and that's their value for the whole first cycle. The 1 gets added for each successive cycle.

So `i` is zero the first time through, `i + 1` is one, and the j-loop causes 1 star to be sent to output before the `print()` skips to the next line. The next time through, `i` is one, and `i + 1` is two, so the j-loop causes 2 stars to be sent to output before `print()`, and so on.

In the following, a pyramid shape is drawn with two additional stars in each succeeding row – one added to the left and one to the right of the preceding row. The challenge here is to put spaces in front of all rows except the last.

Pyramid Pattern [pyramid.py]

```
n = int(input("How many rows to output? "))

stars = 1
skip = n - 1
for i in range(n):
  for j in range(skip): print(" ", end="")
  for j in range(stars): print("*", end="")
  print()
  stars += 2
  skip -= 1
```

Note that there are two additional variables for tracking how many stars to show in each row, and how many spaces to skip before writing the stars. They are separate from the loop counters. Let loop counters be loop counters – if you need something else, declare and manage another variable for whatever that purpose may be.

In any case, the first row has only one star, and each additional row has two more stars than the last – that's why the statement `stars += 2` is there. The number of spaces in front of the first row's star is `n - 1` – you would have to write a star-containing pyramid on paper to figure out this number. The number of skips decreases by one with each successive row, hence the `skip -= 1`.

Finally, note that there are two `j` loops. But since they follow one another, and the first completes before the second begins, it's fine for the second to "recycle" the counter of the first. Also note that the loops are one-liners, and that is a form of a loop that is described in the section 7.6.2 below.

Here is another modification – it reflects the pyramid around its last row to form a diamond shape. All rows except the last are repeated in reverse order.

Diamond Pattern [diamond.py]

```
print("How many rows to output? ", end="")
n = int(input()) # output this many rows

stars = 1
skip = n - 1
for i in range(n):
  for j in range(skip): print(" ", end="")
  for j in range(stars): print("*", end="")
  print()
  stars += 2;
  skip -= 1

stars = 2 * n - 3
skip = 1
extraRows = n - 1
for i in range(extraRows):
  for j in range(skip): print(" ", end="")
  for j in range(stars): print("*", end="")
  print()
  stars -= 2
  skip += 1
```

Note that the two variables for limiting the number of stars and skips are reset so that the first line of the reflection will come out right. Then the `i` loop is modified to cycle one less time, because the last row is not repeated. Then the number of stars *decreases* by 2 and the number of spaces increases by 1 with each reflected row.

Try these, to see the patterns they make! Change the logic to design your own patterns, so that you gain a better understanding of how nested loops work.

7.4.1 A Digital Clock Simulation

This example not only shows *multiple* levels of nesting, but it also demonstrates a few new programming techniques: "sleep" which is useful in computer "simulations" and game programming, the "carriage return" which can be used to overwrite previously displayed output, and automated output formatting.

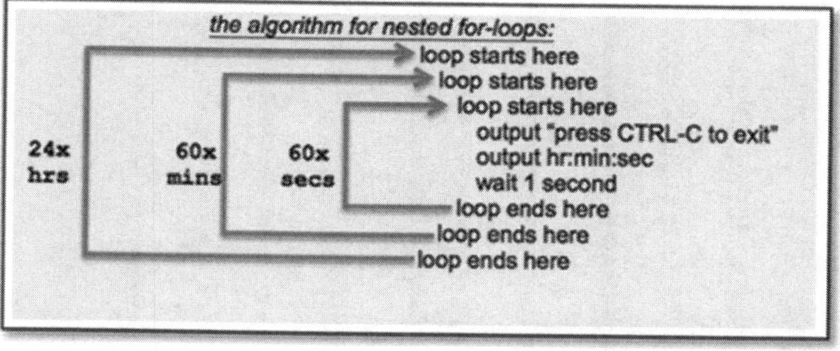

More Nested For-Loops [digitalClock.py]

```
import time

for hour in range(24):
  for minute in range(60):
    for second in range(60):
      print("{:02}".format(hour), end=":")
      print("{:02}".format(minute), end=":")
      print("{:02}".format(second), end="\r")
      time.sleep(1) # sleep for 1 second
```

This example has *three* levels of nesting, requiring *three* counters. It also demonstrates another way to name counters that is more descriptive than `i` and `j`. The outer loop counts hours, so its counter is named `hour`. The innermost loop counts seconds, so its counter is named `second`. The middle loop counts minutes, so its counter is named `minute`. Name counters as you wish, as long as their names follow variable naming rules as explained in chapter 3.

"Sleep" is when a program pauses for a predetermined amount of time, usually measured in seconds. It can be a floating point or whole number.

A carriage return is an old, typewriter term for moving back to the beginning of a line. Sending `'\r'` to output in `print()` gives us a way to overwrite the last output *without* scrolling to the next line like `print()` normally does. The visual effect is that the part of the display being overwritten appears to be animated.

7.5 Two Forms Of The If-Statement

Several different forms of the if-statement have been presented so far, including with and without indented code blocks. This section summarizes the different ways that you can write such statements:

7.5.1 `if` With An Indented Code Block

The most common example has an indented multi-statement code block. When the condition for the if-statement evaluates to *true*, the code block is *not* skipped.

If-Statement With Indented Code Block

```
if ...:
   ...
   ...          one or more
   ...          statements
   ...

# no longer inside the "if"
```

Of course, this form can be used even when there is only one indented statement.

7.5.2 `if` All On One Line

A single-statement code block can also follow the `if` on the same line, condensing the code even further.

One-Line If-Statement
if ...: statement

This is suitable for very short, single statements.

7.6 Two Forms Of Loops

Several examples of loops have been presented so far, nearly all written with indented code blocks, but some as one-liners. This section summarizes the different ways that you can write loops, using `while` and `for`.

7.6.1 Loop With An Indented Code Block

The most common example has an indented multi-statement code block.

Loop With An Indented Code Block

```
while x != 10:
   ...
   ...       one or more
   ...       statements
   ...

# no longer in the loop
```

Actually, this form can be used even when there is only one statement in the code block.

7.6.2 Loop All On One Line

A single-statement code block can also follow the `for` on the same line, condensing the code even further.

One-Line Loop

```
for i in range(10): statement
```

7.7 Advanced Logic Considerations

You'd think that comparison operators and and-logic and or-logic would be all you need for branching and looping, and you're right – *mostly*! There are a couple of situations that arise frequently, that require a bit of thought to figure out. So here are some programming "tricks" to help you deal with them.

7.7.1 Comparing Text

Remember **crossTheRoad.py** in section 6.7.3, where we figured out a way to allow "yes" to be entered as an uppercase "Y" or a lowercase "y"? First we were surprised to find that it even made a difference! Y is Y, right? Well, not necessarily. *Case matters* in programming. "Y" is not "y", and it makes a difference when using them in comparison statements.

We solved that problem in **crossTheRoad.py**, but we totally ignored it in the **thereYet.py** program that preceded it. That's because **thereYet.py** used text input instead of a single character, complicating the matter. So rather than recognize and deal with it, we ignored it. We can ignore it no longer.

In the following example, only the answer "Red" gets checked – that uppercase "R" and lowercase "e" and "d". It's the only version of the word's "casing" that we check.

Testing Input Text [redGreen.py]

```
light = input("What color is the light? [Red/Green]: ")

if light == "Red":
  print("Stop and wait")
```

But what if the user types "red" instead of "Red"? What if the user types "rEd"? In those situations the user will not be warned to stop and wait! This is the issue of "case" – uppercase, lowercase, and "mixed case". We could do `if (light == "red" or light == "Red" or light == "rEd")`, but there are too many combinations for this approach to be practical.

The solution is to read the keyboard input, copy it, and convert the copy to lowercase. Then test the lowercase copy.

the algorithm for testing input text:
ask user to enter color, red or green
create a copy of the user's answer
convert the copy to lowercase
if the converted lowercase copy is "red"
  output "stop"

Testing Input Text [redGreen2.py]

```
light = input("What color is the light? [Red/Green]: ")

if light.lower() == "red":
  print("Stop and wait")
```

The expression `light.lower()` temporarily converts `light` to lowercase. Now the "if" statement needs only to test against the lowercase version of the answer, "red".

7.7.2 Reverse Logic

Logical expressions evaluate to true or false. Sometimes when formulating a logical expression for a programming solution, the logic ends up being the opposite of what was intended. For example, you might come up with "if this condition happens, skip the next code block" when what you really wanted is "if this condition happens, *execute* the next code block". So you would have to reverse the "if" logic. Or you may find it necessary to rewrite a code block in such a way that the originally written logical expression needs to be reformulated as its opposite. For example, the original code block might output "password accepted", but we want to change it to say "invalid password – try again".

There are several different ways to reverse a logical expression, and three of them are presented here. The one you choose depends on the form of the original logical expression.

Using Opposite Operators. If the original expression is a simple comparison with one comparison operator, swap out the operator with its opposite. Swap `==` with `!=`, `<` with `>=`, or `>` with `<=`, and vice versa.

Using "Not" Logic. No matter what the original expression is, you can always enclose it in parentheses and put the keyword "not" in front. So the logical opposite of `if grade == 'A':` is `if not grade == 'A':`. The logical opposite of `if grade == 'A' or grade == 'B' or grade == 'C':` is `if not (grade == 'A' or grade == 'B' or grade == 'C'):` -- note the use of parentheses so that `not` applies to all three `or`s and not just the first one.

Using DeMorgan's Theorem. DeMorgan's Theorem can be applied to expressions that have and-logic or or-logic in them. It is done by swapping `==` with `!=`, `<` with `>=`, or `>` with `<=` (and vise versa), where they appear. Then swap `and` with `or` (and vise versa). For example, the reverse of `answer == 'y' or answer == 'Y'` is `answer != 'y' and answer != 'Y'`. Remember the "True-false Logic WITHOUT Else" code sample from section 7.1? That actually used DeMorgan's Theorem in the second `if`, to get the opposite of the first `if`.

7.8 Exercises, Sample Code, Videos, And Addendums

Go to www.rdb3.com/python/7 for extended materials pertaining to this chapter.

Chapter 8. Simplifying Complicated Programs: Using Functions

Python's subprograms are called "functions". What you need to know about functions is why they are used in programming, the distinction between "void functions" and "value-returning functions", and how "parameter lists" work. You also need to know about two kinds of functions – the ones in Python's modules, and the ones written by you, the programmer. For module functions you need to know the correct `import` to use (if any) in order to have access to a particular function. Note that many of the more common Python module functions do not need `import`. For ones you write, you need to know what are "function definitions" and "function calls", and how to use them.

Things started to get a bit complicated when we introduced validation loops. What used to be a simple code block doubled in size, with a loop and an indented code block. All we wanted to do was transfer one value from the keyboard. It would have been nice to say in one statement: "get a valid value for grade from the keyboard", but it took ten times as many statements with prompts and a loop.

Programs don't have to get too much more complicated than they already are before the code listings get so bogged down in detail that it gets hard to follow the logic. Imagine **itsAboutYou.py** from chapter 5, if we were to add validation to each of its 4 console keyboard inputs – and that program does not even process the inputs or produce any output!

To accommodate this situation, programming languages provide ways to *modularize* code by using "subprograms", or what we're calling "functions" in Python. Remember `math.pow(1 + p, T)` from chapter 4's **amortizationCalc.py**? That uses a function to remove the details of raising a number to a power from the main sequential processing flow. Raising a number to a power is so commonly used that Python already has the function in one of its modules, ready for you to use.

But Python's modules don't have functions to do all the things we would ever want to do. Certainly there are none to validate our example's grade input. We'll learn in this chapter how to write and use our own functions. We'll use them to modularize our programs by removing detailed code blocks from the main sequential processing flow of a program, placing them into separate functions.

8.1 Value-Returning Functions

Let's start with an input validation example that moves the details of input validation into a function.

Look for these three main parts *inside* the function, because they provide beginning programmers with a formula for success when learning to write their own value-returning functions. You can eventually stray from this exact formulation, as most programmers do, but not until you know *exactly* what you are doing!

3 Parts Of A Value-Returning Function
1. Declare a variable named `result` with a default value. 2. Write code to possibly reassign a different value to `result`, replacing its default value. 3. "Return" `result`.

Input Validation With A Value-Returning Function [passingGradeFun.py]

```
def getGrade():
  # step 1
  result = 'X' # the default value

  # step 2
  while True:
    result = input("What is your grade? [A, B, C, D, F, or X to quit]: ")[0]

    if result == 'A' or result == 'B' or result == 'C': break
    if result == 'D' or result == 'F': break
    if result == 'X' or result == 'x': break

    print(result, "is not a valid grade. Try again...")

  # step 3
  return result
# getGrade ends here

# main program starts here
while True:
  grade = getGrade()
  if grade == 'X' or grade == 'x': break;
  if grade == 'A' or grade == 'B' or grade == 'C':
    print("You pass")

print("Thanks for checking your grades!")
```

Okay – so it does not *look* less complicated than it did before without functions. But if you look at what we'll now call the "main program", you will notice that *it* is simpler. The code for prompting the user and the loop for validating the input are all replaced with one statement, `grade = getGrade()`.

Let's take apart the above example in order to understand how value-returning functions work.

8.1.1 The Function Call

`getGrade()` is a function call. It is an *expression* that invokes the function, suspending the main program's sequential processing flow until the function finishes. The call resolves to a value, just as if it was a variable name, and since it is used in an assignment statement, that value gets stored in the variable `grade`.

Function names follow the same rules for identifiers as variables do. So how can Python tell that `getGrade` is a function and not a variable? It can tell because functions have parentheses after the identifier and variables do not. While `grade = getGrade()` is a function call, `grade = getGrade` would expect `getGrade` to represent a variable (which it does not!)

Actually, the same function call can be used in programs more than once, if you have the need to do so. A call can be used anywhere that you would otherwise use a value, variable, or expression – even inside the body of its own "definition" (yikes!) But in our case, we only need it once (whew!)

8.1.2 The Function Definition

Function definitions are normally placed after any `import` statement(s) and before what we're now calling the "main program". It has a "header" that starts with the Python keyword `def`. The header also has the function's name with parentheses and a colon symbol, like this: `def getGrade():`.

After the header is the body of the function in one or more indented code blocks. This is the detailed code that got removed from the main program, where it was replaced by a function call. It gets run whenever a call is made that references it by the function's name.

8.1.3 The `return` Statement

Value-returning functions are distinguished from the other type of functions (void) because they have a `return` statement as the last statement in its body. Following the keyword "return", there needs to be a value, variable, or expression. In our case, it will usually be `return result`.

8.1.4 The Scope Of Variables Owned By Functions

Thinking back to the discussion about "scope" in 6.7.4, why does a function have to "return" anything? Can't the main program "see" the variables that get declared inside the function's body? No – they are locally owned, private property of the function! So for anything from a function to get back to the main program, that function has to explicitly return it. So that's where value-returning functions get their name.

8.2 Parameter Lists

Note that the parentheses of `getGrade` are empty in **passingGradeFun.py**. But the parentheses of `math.pow` are *not* empty in **amortizationCalc.py** from chapter 4. A function's parentheses identify it as a function instead of a variable. But they also are a container for *inputs* to the function. It is a way for the call to send values to the function for processing. The function call `math.pow(1 + p, T)` has two inputs separated by commas. This list of comma-separated inputs is called the "parameter list".

If a function has empty parentheses, then it has no inputs, like `getGrade`. The number and type of the values in the parameter list of a call *must* match what the function expects them to be. This is specified in the "header". So since the header for `getGrade` has empty parentheses, the call must have empty parentheses, too.

In the `math.pow` calls, the expression `1 + p` is resolved first, by retrieving the value stored in `p` and adding 1 to it. Then the value stored in `T` is retrieved, and these two values are "sent" to the function. The following example shows how to write and use a function with a *non-empty* parameter list:

Using A Function Parameter List [paramList.py]

```
def calcAverage(a, b):
  result = 0 # step 1
  result = (a + b) / 2 # step 2
  return result # step 3
# calcAverage ends here

# main program starts here
x = 100
y = 200
z = calcAverage(x, y)
print(z)
```

Note that each input in the header's parameter list has a data type and an identifier. The data type specifies what the value, variable, or expression in the call has to conform to. Each identifier, `a` and `b`, is a variable for use *inside* the function, initialized to the value from the call, `calcAverage(x, y)`.

When the program starts at the first statement in the main program, and the sequential processing of statements reaches the one with the call, here is what happens. The values stored in `x` and `y` are retrieved and used to initialize the values of `a` and `b` in the function. Then the function's code is processed, and a value for the variable `result` is determined. When the function ends, it substitutes the value stored in `result` for the expression `calcAverage(x, y)` in main. Then sequential processing continues in the main program.

It is important to remember that parameters in calls are evaluated as values, and they are used to initialize the variables in the function's parameter list. That is why calls can have values, variables, or expressions, because they all can be reduced to values before the call takes place.

Note how the variable names in main do not match those in `calcAverage` – they do not have to. It is not their names that determine how they transfer their values to the function – it is their location in the parameter list that does.

Also note that the setting of `result` to a default value of zero is not really necessary. In fact, the body of the function could be written any of these ways:

Alternative Ways To Write `calcAverage`	

`result = 0 # a default`
`result = (a + b) / 2`
`return result`
	`return (a + b) / 2`

`result = (a + b) / 2` `return result`	`return ((a + b) / 2)`

8.3 Void Functions

Sometimes functions produce their own output and do not need to return anything to the main program. In this case, there is no `return` statement to return a value. Here's a simplified example of what is called a "void function":

A Simple Void Function [name.py]

```
def outputName(name):
  print(name)
# outputName ends here

# main program starts here
outputName("George Washington")
```

The most important thing to remember about void functions is that the call must be made as a *stand-alone statement* – it cannot be used as an expression in another statement. That is because it does not produce a value that can be substituted for the call. So the call statement looks like this: `outputName("George Washington")`. Note also that there is no `return` statement in the function, and no 3-step process like we have in value-returning functions.

Besides demonstrating how void functions work, this example also shows that text can be passed through a parameter list, and that actual values can be substituted for variables in a function call.

The next example shows how a function can be called more than once:

Using Void Functions [addition.py]

```
def additionProblem(topNumber, bottomNumber):
  print("\n\n\n      ", topNumber, "+", bottomNumber, "= ", end = "")
  userAnswer = int(input())

  theAnswer = topNumber + bottomNumber
  if theAnswer == userAnswer:
    print("      Correct!")
  else:
    print("      Very good, but a better answer is", theAnswer)
# additionProblem ends here

# main program starts here
additionProblem(8, 2)
additionProblem(4, 8)
additionProblem(3, 7)
additionProblem(4, 10)
additionProblem(11, 2)
```

Note the text containing three `\n`s. "Backslash-N" inside quoted text is another was to skip to the next line besides using several `print()`s.

8.3.1 Using `return` In Void Functions

While value-returning functions *do* have to end with a `return` statement, and void functions do *not*, it's actually possible to see `return` in a void function. It's used to exit a void function before reaching the end of it. But to distinguish it from a value-returning function, it's just **return** without specifying a return value. And it's never needed at the end of the function.

8.3.2 Randomizing Functions And Game Programming

The math problems in the above example are specified by the programmer. Every time the program runs, it presents the same 5 problems. It would be nice if the computer could choose the numbers for the problems at random!

Python provides a "random number generator". To randomly "draw" a whole number with a value between 0 and 9, inclusive, use this expression:

```
random.randint(0, 9)
```

Each result is equally probable. Here's how to simulate the roll of a six-sided die:

```
random.randint(1, 6)
```

Here's how to simulate the roll of two six-sided dice:

```
random.randint(1, 6) + random.randint(1, 6)
```

Use of random numbers in Python requires the module: `import random`.

8.4 Some Examples With Functions

Here are some examples with functions. You can copy, save, and run them. You can modify them and see how they work. Make sure that you understand everything in each of these examples.

8.4.1 Input Validation Example

Here's an example of a validating input loop in a function:

An Input Validation Function [yesNo.py]

```
def getAnswer():
  result = "" # step 1

  while True:
    result = input("Your answer [yes/no]: ")
    if result == "yes": break
    if result == "no": break
    print("Let's try this again.")

  return result # step 3
# getAnswer ends here

# main program starts here
...do stuff...
if getAnswer() == "yes":
  ...do stuff...
```

8.4.2 A Password-Protected Program

Here's an example that shows how to password-protect a program:

A Password-Protected Program [password.py]

```
def getPassword():
  while True:
    password = input("Enter the password: ")
    if password == "12345": break
    print("INVALID. ", end = "")
# getPassword ends here

# main program starts here
getPassword()
...do stuff...
```

8.4.3 Void vs Value-Returning

Here is an example that converts the void function in **addition.py** into a value-returning function in order to keep score. Some programmers will write a value-returning function where a void function would otherwise do, so that it can return a *result code*. A result code value of zero usually indicates success. Any other value can be used as an error code.

In the example below, a value of one is returned if the answer is correct, so that it can be added to the score in main.

Using A Value-Returning Function Instead Of Void [keepingScore.py]

```
import random

def additionProblem(topNumber, bottomNumber):
  result = 0 #step 1

  print("\n\n\n     ", topNumber, "+", bottomNumber, "= ", end = "")
  userAnswer = int(input())

  theAnswer = topNumber + bottomNumber
  if theAnswer == userAnswer:
    print("      Correct!")
    result = 1
  else:
    print("      Very good, but a better answer is", theAnswer)

  return result #step 3
# additionProblem ends here

# main program starts here
score = 0
score += additionProblem(random.randint(0, 9), random.randint(0, 9))
score += additionProblem(random.randint(0, 9), random.randint(0, 9))
score += additionProblem(random.randint(0, 9), random.randint(0, 9))
score += additionProblem(random.randint(0, 9), random.randint(0, 9))
score += additionProblem(random.randint(0, 9), random.randint(0, 9))

print("\n      TOTAL SCORE:", score, "out of 5")
```

Note that the above example also puts in the random element, so that the problems are different every time the program runs. Also note that it introduces a shorthand way to write `score = score + ...`, which is `score += ...`. (Actually, since the 5 statements in main are exactly the same, we could have put in a count-controlled loop and written the statement only once!)

The `+=` operator introduced in the above example has some relatives. Here is a list of some useful shorthand operators, by example:

Shorthand Operator Example:	...Is Shorthand For:
`score += 1`	`score = score + 1`
`score -= 1`	`score = score - 1`
`result *= 10`	`result = result * 10`
`average /= n`	`average = average / n`

8.5 Classic Computer Science Solutions

The two classic problems introduced in chapter 6 lend themselves well to solutions with functions. We still have to get to chapter 11 to complete these solutions, but we can move closer to them here.

8.5.1 Classic Min/Max Solution In A Function

The classic problem of finding the minimum and/or maximum values from among multiple values can be solved with functions. This lets the details of the logic be removed and reused. Here are some code blocks that show how this is done:

Finding The Maximum Or Minimum Value

```
def getMaxValue(a, b, c):
  result = a
  if result < b: result = b
  if result < c: result = c
  return result
# getMaxValue ends here

def getMinValue(a, b, c):
  result = a
  if result > b: result = b
  if result > c: result = c
  return result
# getMinValue ends here
```

To extend this to 4 or more values, just add more parameters and more if-statements.

8.5.2 Classic Sorting Logic

The classic problem of reordering multiple values from lowest to highest (or the reverse) can also be handled with functions. While we need to get through chapter 11 before we can fully deal with this problem, we can get closer here.

Sorting Values Lo-to-Hi

```
def sortValues(a, b, c):

  # move the lowest value to "a"
  if a > b: a,b = b,a
  if a > c: a,c = c,a

  # move the next lowest value to "b"
  if b > c: b,c = c,b

  # output the reordered values
  print(a, b, c, sep = ", ")

# sortValues ends here
```

Since the parameter values are shared with the function as *copies* of their original values, the originals in the call statement are not affected. This function can be adapted to variables of other data types, as well.

8.6 Exercises, Sample Code, Videos, And Addendums

Go to www.rdb3.com/python/8 for extended materials pertaining to this chapter.

Chapter 9. Counting On Your Fingers: Bits And Bytes

What you need to know about computer memory is how numbers and text are stored, which will help you understand why numbers and text are treated separately in programming. You also need to understand why there is a distinction between whole numbers and floating point numbers, and to know that there is a *precision issue* with floating point variables.

We know that computers can store values, including numbers and text – even audio and video. But just how do they do that, anyway? This chapter explains how computers store values, and in so doing, shows why computers make the distinction between whole numbers and floating point numbers. And in case you've been thinking that all we need is the `float()` conversion and why should we ever use `int()`, this chapter will help you see the value of `int()`.

9.1 Computer Memory: Vast Arrays Of On/Off Switches

If you study the "memory" of a computer – what's inside those SD cards, memory sticks, and DDRs – you will find that they consist of millions or billions of electronic on/off switches. That's it – nothing more than on/off switches. Each switch can store one of two possible values – off or on – zero or one.

A switch is called a *bit*, and it is made out of several electrical components – resistors and transistors combined in a circuit. By applying an electrical pulse to the circuit that comprises one bit, it can be placed into one of two possible states, which represent "on" and "off".

So how can a computer store a number, which has many more than two possible values? Well, remember when you learned to count on your fingers? Each finger can be held up or down to represent on or off. By combining all ten fingers of both hands, you could group fingers in various ways to represent numbers in the range of 0 to 10. Computers do something like this.

9.1.1 Bits And Counting

Computers group bits together in order to get past the zero-one range limitation. Just like our hands group our fingers in sets of five, computers (typically) group bits in sets of eight – a set of 8 bits is called a *byte.*

On the fingers of one hand you learned to count from zero to five, and so you might think that a byte can be used to count from zero to eight. But computer designers realized that we were not using our 5 fingers very efficiently. Consider this: there are multiple ways to represent the number *two*, depending on which two fingers you hold up – what a waste! What if every possible combination of fingers held up or down represented a different number? There are 32 (that is, 2 x 2 x 2 x 2 x 2) unique combinations, ranging from all fingers down to all fingers up. We could actually count from 0 to 31 on the fingers of one hand, if we assigned a unique number to each unique finger configuration. (Pinky-up could be 1, ring-finger-up could be 2, pinky-up and index-finger-up could be 9, etc.) Extend this idea to two hands, and we can count to over 1000 – now that's efficiency!

Here's how to do this: assign the value 1 to your pinky, 2 to your ring finger, 4 to your middle finger, 8 to your index finger, and 16 to your thumb. (The key is to start with 1 and double it each time). For any finger held up, add its value to the total. For example, pinky and ring finger both up is 3 (that is, 1 + 2). (Since some up-down finger combinations are painful or impossible, you might try holding your open hand over a flat surface, and touching the surface to represent "up" – it's easier and faster to do.)

9.1.2 Bits And Negative Numbers

So our hand can simulate a byte of computer memory, and store numbers from 0 to 31 or more, depending on how many hands we use. But what about negative numbers? There is one obvious solution – use one finger to track whether the number is positive or negative – a "sign bit". But this idea is just a little bit wasteful, because it results in two ways to represent zero – plus zero and minus zero! A *better* solution is to make the largest bit represent the *negative* of its normal value. That is, let the thumb in a one-hand number be -16 instead of +16. Then all fingers except the thumb up represents 15 (that is, 1 + 2 + 4 + 8), thumb up only represents -16, thumb and pinky is -15, etc.

If we were to use two hands, the 16 thumb would go back to +16, and the thumb of the *second* hand would go negative (-512, actually).

Whole numbers are done this way in computers. Python represents whole numbers using as many bytes as it needs. If you are used to C or C++ or Java, this is a whole new concept, because in those languages, the number of bytes for any given number is determined in advance with a limited number of options, resulting in range limitation issues. Not so in Python!

So we can represent whole numbers in computer memory. But what about *fractions*?

9.2 Floating Point Numbers

The use of bytes to represent numbers does not address fractional values. There's a 1 and a 2, but what about 1½? What about 3.14159265? A solution is to modify the bit-counting approach so that instead of representing whole numbers, we represent fractional values instead. That is, the pinky's value is ½, ring finger is 1, index finger is 2, etc. – or we could start with ¼ or less for the pinky. This is *almost* what the computer does, and for this to work, there needs to be a second set of data types – ones whose first bit is a fraction instead of 1. (Actually, the value of the first bit varies, depending on the size of the value being stored – for example, why stop at ¼ if the number stored is only 10?)

But no matter how many bytes Python adds to track a floating point value, each time it cuts an interval in half, there's still a continuum of values between adjacent fractions. And that results in a *precision* problem.

If computers are so accurate, why are we talking about precision? Consider the case where the pinky value is ½. We can only represent values *to the nearest half.* And even though the first bit in a floating point representation is effectively a lot smaller than ½, the problem remains – there is *no continuum of numbers* on the computer's number line! So if we divide our hand-held number of 1½ by two, we should get ¾ – but we cannot divide numbers finely enough to show the ¼ value – we have ½ and 1, and that's as close as we can get to ¾. We end up *rounding off* the true number to one that is as close as we can get in computer's numbering system. Try the following code block for yourself:

Round-Off Error

```
# try this in Python
x = 1 / 3
xFormatted2 = "%.2f" % x
xFormatted20 = "%.20f" % x

print(xFormatted2, xFormatted20)
```

If you run the above code you should see that the output for the value rounded to 2 decimal digits works fine – it's 0.33. But the one rounded to 20 decimal digits, which one would expect to show 20 threes, does *not* do so! After 15 or so threes it drifts off. This is commonly called "round-off error", although technically it's not an error – it's just how computers work. Note that `x` itself is unaffected by this "error".

Want to see more? Try this – after setting `x` to one third and before getting the two formatted versions of it, add one million to `x` like this: `x += 1000000`. Now see what you get for output!

Precision is an issue for floating point numbers, but not for whole numbers. *That is why we have both* – so we can choose the precision of whole numbers at the expense of fractional capabilities, or choose the fractional capabilities of floating points at the expense of precision. It's an age-old result of the way computers work, and is *not* particular to Python – it's due to the fact that computers are digital entities and they count on their "fingers".

9.2.1 Output Precision vs Floating Point Precision

Wait a minute – we were able to specify the precision for `x` in the last example with `"%.2f" % x` and `"%.20f" % x`. Shouldn't that give the programmer some control over this issue of precision? Well, obviously not, judging by the results of the example! It turns out that these simply direct that the output be *displayed* with the number of decimal digits specified. If the number is stored with *less* precision than is asked for in the output, the computer "makes up" the digits that it does not know exactly! (It's better than generating a error and terminating the program at that point.)

Try this – the loops *should* each cycle 10 times. But one of them actually goes on forever!

More Round-Off Error	
This Stops When It Should.	This Does Not!

`x = 0`
`while x != 1:`
`  print(x)`
`  x += 0.125`
	`x = 0`
	`while x != 1:`
	`  print(x)`
	`  x += 0.1`

9.3 Representing Characters

Bits are used in various combinations to represent whole numbers and floating point numbers. But what about characters and text? The solution is actually a simple one – numbers are used to stand for characters, and the *data type* distinguishes between the two. For example, the number 65 when viewed as a whole number is 65, but when viewed as a character it's A.

There are enough characters in Python to cover all the languages of the world! The first 128 in the sequence are called the "ASCII standard" characters. They include the English alphabet, punctuation symbols, and "control characters" like end-of-line. They are a throwback to a time when computer memory was *very* limited and every bit counted. Beyond ASCII is the modern Unicode character set.

In case you are wondering, ASCII stands for "American Standard Code for Information Interchange". You may also be wondering since characters are represented by numbers, what happens if you add or subtract from a character? That is, for `x = 'A'`, what does the expression `x += 1` do? It advances the character to the next one in the ASCII sequence, `'B'` (code 66)! So the following code block outputs the alphabet – note the conversions back and forth between character representations and their numeric equivalents with the `ord` and `chr` functions:

Output The English Alphabet

```
x = ord("A") # get numeric equivalent of A
while x <= ord("Z"):
  print(chr(x), end = " ") # convert number to character
  x += 1 # "bump" the number to the next character
print()
```

9.4 The True/False, Yes/No, On/Off, Up/Down, Left/Right Data Type

There is another type of value that is separate from numbers and text. It is the only thing that a bit can represent by itself: two exact opposites. Ironically, since bits are grouped as bytes in computer memory, it still takes a whole byte's worth of bits to do this. After all, to use just one finger, you still have to involve a whole hand! This data type is a "Boolean".

Booleans are used as "flags". Its two possible values are `True` and `False`. No, there are not any "yes", "no", "left", or "right" values – you just have to decide which of a pair of opposites is to be represented by `True` and which is `False`.

For example, we will search through sets of data in following chapters, and we will use a Boolean result to tell whether or not we found a specific value in the data set. Here's an incomplete sample code block:

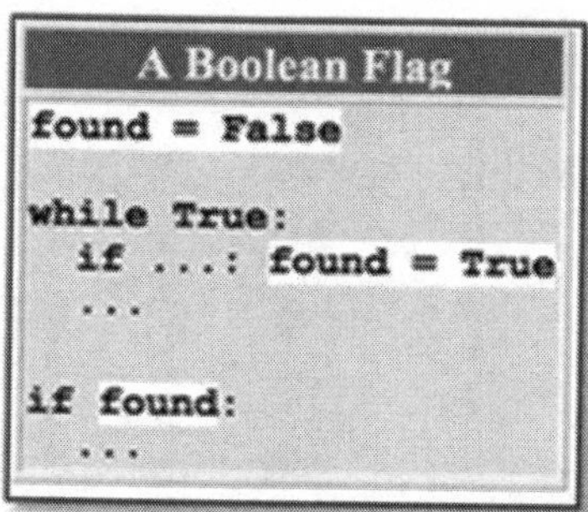

A Boolean Flag

```
found = False

while True:
  if ...: found = True
  ...

if found:
  ...
```

Booleans also offer a more straightforward way of writing 8.4.3's **keepingScoreBoolean.py**:

Using A Boolean As A Return Type [keepingScoreBool.py]

```
import random

def additionProblem(topNumber, bottomNumber):
  result = False #step 1

  print("\n\n\n     ", topNumber, "+", bottomNumber, "= ", end = "")
  userAnswer = int(input())

  theAnswer = topNumber + bottomNumber
  if theAnswer == userAnswer:
    print("      Correct!")
    result = True
  else:
    print("      Very good, but a better answer is", theAnswer)

  return result #step 3
# additionProblem ends here

# main program starts here
score = 0
if additionProblem(random.randint(0, 9), random.randint(0, 9)): score += 1
if additionProblem(random.randint(0, 9), random.randint(0, 9)): score += 1
if additionProblem(random.randint(0, 9), random.randint(0, 9)): score += 1
if additionProblem(random.randint(0, 9), random.randint(0, 9)): score += 1
if additionProblem(random.randint(0, 9), random.randint(0, 9)): score += 1

print("\n      TOTAL SCORE:", score, "out of 5")
```

Also note that the if-statements in the main program all have their associated one-statement code blocks at the end, rather than indented on the next line. This is okay, and it is done here because it is easier to read.

And like before, the `if additionProblem(random.randint(0, 9), random.randint(0, 9)): score += 1` statement appears five times, each exactly the same – no reason that could not have been put into a for-loop!

9.5 Literal Values

Values written directly into code are called *literal values.* Depending on how they are written, they have a data type associated with them. For example, whole numbers are as if they were returned by the `int()` function (like `0`, `100`, or `-1`). Floating point numbers are as if they were returned by the `float()` function (like `0.0`, `3.14159`, or `-40.0`).

Literals are usually base 10 numbers, but whole number literals can also be octal (base 8) or hexadecimal (base 16). To write a number as base 8 octal, prepend a zero oh (like `0o11`, which is the same as decimal 9, or `0o77` which is the same as decimal 63 – 7 eights plus 7 ones). Note that 0o8 and 0o9 are undefined and will cause errors, because the digits 8 and 9 do not exist in base 8. To write a number as base 16 hexadecimal, prepend 0x (like `0xFFFF` or `0xABCD1234`). Note that A through F are digits added to the base 10 set of 0 through 9 in order to get 16 digits for the base 16 numbering system.

Literal text values are written as *any* number of characters, with a matching pair of single- or double-quote marks before and after (like `"Hello"` or `'Goodbye'`). Literal Boolean values are `True` and `False`.

9.6 Type Conversion

Computer languages have a variety of ways to store value, and each variable in your program uses one of them at a time. Also, the result of an operation (like addition) depends on whether values being operated on are numbers or text. Here's the problem: if you input 3 numbers (stored for example in `a`, `b`, and `c`) without using `int()` or `float()` and you want their total, the expression `a + b + c` will join the digit characters! Not what you expected.

The solution to this problem is *type conversion*. Here's how – the variables' contents are not affected, but the results of the conversion expressions are treated as if they were numbers:

Type Conversion Expressions: Text To Number

```
a = input("a=") # enter for example, 123
b = input("b=") # enter for example, 3.14
c = input("c=") # enter for example, -100

total = a + b + c # for example, 1233.14-100
total = float(a) + float(b) + float(c) # for example, 26.14
total = int(a) + float(b) + int(c) # this works, too
```

Remember `chr()` and `ord()` from section 9.3, where we converted between characters and their numeric codes? That was type conversion. And if you ever *did* want to join the digits in numbers as if they were text, it's like this:

Type Conversion Expressions: Number To Text

```
a = 40
b = 24
c = a + b # the result is 64

asText = a + " + " + b + " = " + c # does NOT work
asText = str(a) + " + " + str(b) + " = " + str(c) # this does
```

9.6.1 Changing A Variable's Type

In Python you can even change a variable from text to a number, or number to text:

Type Conversion Statements

```
a = 40 # a literal whole number
b = "100" # literal text

a = str(a) # now it's "40"
b = int(b) # now it's 100
```

9.7 Exercises, Sample Code, Videos, And Addendums

Go to www.rdb3.com/python/9 for extended materials pertaining to this chapter.

Chapter 10. Interactive Programs: File I/O

Input can be gathered from a variety of sources. In chapters 3 and 4 we specified input values directly in the program listings. Then in chapter 5 we learned how to get values from a user via the `input` function. In this chapter we learn how to get user-typed input from a text file, so a user can stage their input values in advance of running the program, and save and edit them in a file. The same techniques can be applied to save the scores in computer games – how many wins and how many losses!

10.1 Text File Input

Text files are like typing responses to console prompts, but doing so in advance and storing them in a file. It's remarkably easy to convert console input to text file input. Actually, you can "mix-and-match" file and console input in the same program, so that there can be some of each. For example, you could use console input for a user to type the name of a text file, and then get the rest of the input from that text file.

But there are two important differences between console input and text file input. Prompts are not necessary for text file input – remember, the responses are typed in advance and stored in a text file. So the user has to know the program pretty well in order to know what to reply *before* the questions are asked! Another difference is that the *name* of a file has to be specified, and your program has to "open" the file.

The coding requirements for text file input are these: (1) an "object" to manage the file, (2) Python's `open` function to open a named file for the object to manage, and (3) a replacement for the console's `input` function call: `readline`.

10.1.1 The `fin` Object

So far we've used variables only for numbers and text. But variables in modern computer languages are more versatile than that – they can store "objects", too. Objects can do some pretty complex things. In the same way, a human brain can remember a simple number, while the same brain can remember how to factor a polynomial. Variables can store numbers, and can even store the complex steps to a solution that somebody else already figured out – like how to interact with a file on a computer drive.

Here's an example of how to create an object that can interact with a file for input. It uses a variable named `fin`:

```
fin = open("data.txt")
```

Actually, the variable does not have to be named `fin` – it just has to be any valid identifier. Here it stands for "file input".

"Opening" a file makes an exclusive, read-only attachment of a specified file to your program. This attachment continues until your program "closes" the file or ends.

You do not *have* to close a file that your program has opened – it closes automatically when your program ends. But it's a good programming practice to write a "close" statement just as soon as you are done with a file. It's like the best time to close the refrigerator door is when you are done taking stuff out or putting stuff in – don't wait until after lunch to go back to the kitchen and close it!

Likewise, after the last reference to `fin`, when you are finished reading from the file, use this statement to close the file:

```
fin.close()
```

10.1.2 More Ways To Open Files

Above, the name of the file to be opened is **data.txt**. It is expected to exist in the *working* folder. You can specify that a file be located in any other folder by including the folder specification in front of the filename, like this *(note the forward slash* `/` *– some systems also allow a backslash, but it has to be written as a double-backslash:* `\\`*)*:

```
fin = open("e:/python/data.txt")
```

The filename does *not* have to end in **.txt**. It can be anything, including **.ini** or no filename extension at all. The only requirement is that it be a text file – one that is editable and viewable using any text editor. The other type of file is "binary" – that's left for future study.

The filename can be specified using a text variable instead of a filename written in quotes, like this:

```
fileName = "e:/python/data.txt"
fin = open(fileName)
```

Since you can use a text variable to specify the filename in an "open" statement, that makes it possible to prompt the user to type the name of a file:

```
fileName = input("What file do you want to use for input? ")
fin = open(fileName)
```

Note that you may include a folder specification for a file when you type it in response to a prompt. Use either a universally understood slash `/` or a Windows backslash `\` to separate parent and child folders – you do *not* have to use double-backslash as you would do if you typed the filename in your code.

To read a file a second time, close it and open it again. Here's how to reopen the same file, or use `fin` to open a different file:

```
fin.close()
fileName = input("What file do you want to use for input next? ")
fin = open(fileName)
```

Here's a handy table of interchangeable code blocks for opening a text file for input, summarizing the preceding discussion:

fin = open Variations

```
fin = open("data.txt") # in the working folder

# open a specifically named file, data.txt, in some other folder
fin = open("e:/python/data.txt") # PC
fin = open("/Volumes/programming/python/data.txt") # Mac

# open a file whose name is stored in a text variable
fileName = "e:/python/data.txt" # PC
fileName = "/Volumes/programming/python/data.txt" # Mac
fin = open(fileName)

# open a file whose name is entered by the user
fileName = input("What file do you want to use for input? ")
fin = open(fileName)

# open a 2nd file (storing the filename in a text variable)
fin.close() # close 1st file before opening 2nd
fileName = input("What file do you want to use for input next? ")
fin = open(fileName)
```

10.1.3 Error Handling

File error handling is *not* required in Python. The purpose of writing error-handling code is to tell the computer what to do *in case* there is a problem with file I/O. To accommodate possible file I/O errors, use a try-except code block. It works like this:

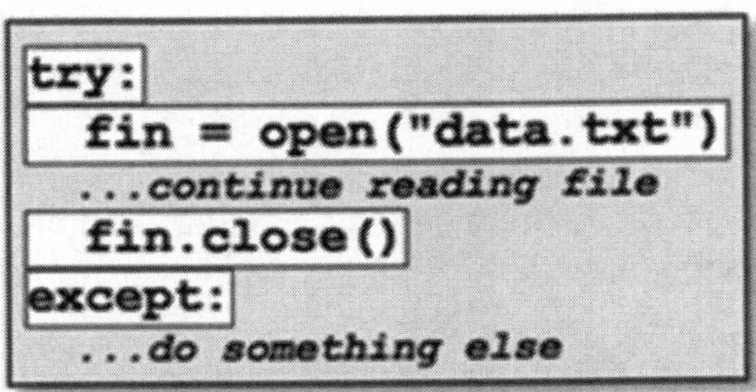

```
try:
   fin = open("data.txt")
   ...continue reading file
   fin.close()
except:
   ...do something else
```

10.1.4 Bringing It All Together: File Input Coding

Here is an example that converts section 5.1's **itsAboutYou.py** program to use file input – note that `input()` is simply replaced by `fin.readline().strip()`:

Transferring Values From A Text File [itsAboutYou2.py]

```
try:
  fin = open("aboutYou.txt")

  # read a whole number from one line of an input file
  age = int(fin.readline().strip()) # store as a whole number

  # read a floating point number from one line of an input file
  gpa = float(fin.readline().strip()) # store as a floating point number

  # read text from one line of an input
  name = fin.readline().strip() # store as text

  # read a single character from one line of an input file
  gender = fin.readline().strip()[0] # store as a single character

  fin.close()

except:
  print("file not found")
```

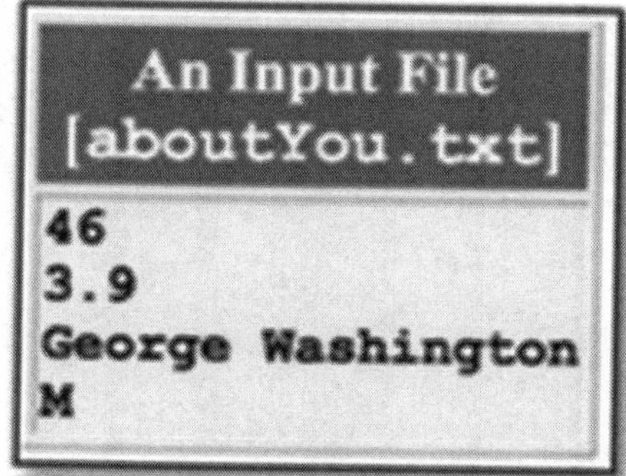

An Input File [aboutYou.txt]

```
46
3.9
George Washington
M
```

Of course, the above program produces no output. But by leaving out this detail, we can focus on text file input coding. Note how similar it is to console input – one uses `input()` and the other uses `fin.readline().strip()`. Also note the differences – text file input requires that the filename be specified in an `open` statement, and has no prompts.

In file input, the statement that "reads" an input value also skips to the next input value in the file – that is, it reads it sequentially. There is no need to write any code to advance to the next input value, because this happens automatically. There is also no going back or skipping forward – not easily, anyway. The most straightforward way to go back to a previous input is to close and reopen the text file.

10.1.5 End-Of-File Loops

To process *all* of the input in a text file without knowing in advance the number of lines in the file, there a special end-of-file for-loop. It replaces the `fin.readline()` sequence with `lineFromFile`, which itself gets defined in the for-loop:

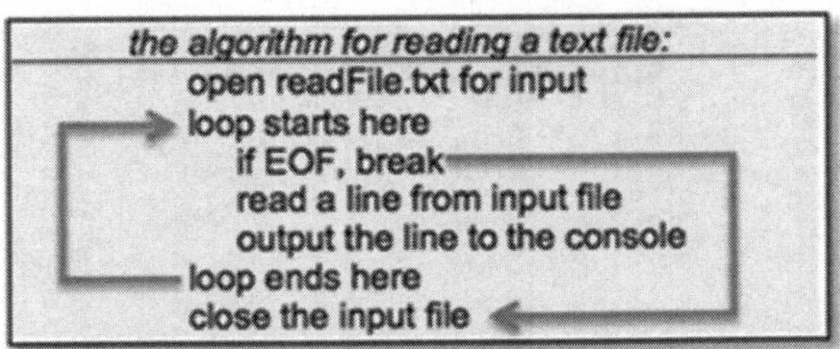

the algorithm for reading a text file:
open readFile.txt for input
loop starts here
if EOF, break
read a line from input file
output the line to the console
loop ends here
close the input file

Reading A Text File With A End-Of-File Loop [readFile.py]

```
try:
  fin = open("readFile.txt")

  for lineFromFile in fin:
    name = lineFromFile.strip()
    print(name)

  fin.close()

except:
  print("file not found")
```

In the above example, the loop automatically detects when the end of the file is reached, and breaks. And actually there is nothing special about the name `lineFromFile` – it's just a variable's name, which can be any valid Python variable name you choose. It stores the text of one line, *with* that line's line break character at the end, `\n`. That's what `.strip()` does – it removes the line break. `lineFromFile` is reusable, too – when the loop goes to its next cycle, `lineFromFile` forgets what it used to store, and goes on to store the text of the next line in the file.

10.2 Text File Output

Sending output to a text file involves the use of a slightly different kind of object – one that outputs to a file instead of reading it. While we can store the object in any named variable, we choose the name `fout`, for "file output". Here is how to open a named file using `fout` – the `"w"` is for "write":

```
fout = open("data.txt", "w")
```

Outputting to a text file is a lot like sending output to the console screen. Instead of `print`, it uses `fout.write`. And as with file input, it's a good idea to close the file as soon as you're done outputting to it. But if you don't, the program will close it automatically when it ends.

There's just two things about `fout.write` that you need to know – it's like `print` with `end = ""` already in it. That's fine if you want to build a line in the output file with multiple output statements, but what if you really want to skip to the next line? That's where the `\n` line break symbol comes in, as you'll see in the sample code below. It first appeared in 6.7.2 to skip lines on the console screen.

The other thing about `fout.write` is that it only writes text – no numbers! And it only writes *one* thing – no commas in its parentheses. So it's a good thing we covered type conversion already in chapter 9. You'll see how this works in the coming sample code.

10.2.1 The `fout` Object

As with `fin`, this does not have to be named `fout` – it just has to be any valid identifier.

When specifying a filename to receive output, the file may either already exist or not. If you specify a file that already exists, the file will be discarded and overwritten *without warning*. If the file does not already exist, this process creates it. In most operating systems it will appear in the file listing as soon as it is opened for output, but its size may be reported as zero until it is closed or the program ends.

Then after the last reference to **fout**, when you are finished writing to the file, use this statement to close the file:

```
fout.close()
```

In the above, **data.txt** will be created (or recreated) in the *working* folder. As with input files, you can specify that a file be located in any other folder by including the folder specification in front of the filename. Also, the filename does *not* have to end in **.txt**. The text file that is written by your program will be editable and viewable using any text editor.

Overwriting of files is useful if you are keeping score in a game, or saving the state of a program for later restart at the same position. For example, a tic-tac-toe game may save the number of wins, losses, and ties in a text file. Upon starting the game, the program could read the file and display the win-loss history. While playing the game, the win-loss history is updated by new wins and losses. Then when the program ends, it replaces the old win-loss history file by overwriting it.

Here is an example that uses a text file to keep score. To keep it simple, the program itself does not control the game being played – it just keeps score:

Keeping Score [keepingScore2.py]

```
scoreFile = "scores.txt"

# read past scores (or initialize to zero)
try:
  fin = open(scoreFile)
  wins = int(fin.readline().strip())
  losses = int(fin.readline().strip())
  print("You won", wins, "time(s).")
  print("You lost", losses, "time(s).")
  fin.close()
except:
  wins = 0
  losses = 0

# play the game(s) in a loop here (MISSING)
# ...for each win, do wins++;
# ...for each loss, do losses++;

# rewrite scores.txt with the latest scores
fout = open(scoreFile, "w")
fout.write(str(wins) + "\n")
fout.write(str(losses) + "\n")
fout.close()
```

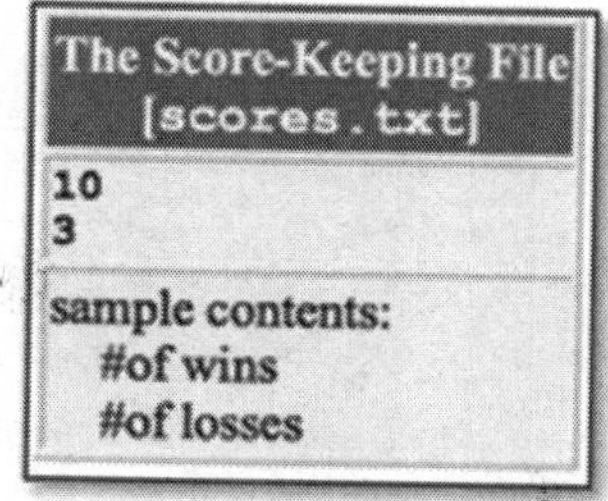

The above program uses a variable `scoreFile` to store the name of the text file. This is an alternative to typing the exact same name twice, in the two file opening statements (one for input and another for output). It is good programming practice to store a recurring value in a variable and use the variable instead of repeating the value.

Study the above code listing, because there are some subtleties – see if you can identify and understand each:

- Blank lines are used to separate blocks of code, making it easier for humans to read – it makes no difference to Python.
- The `.close()` statements appear as soon as they possibly can. This is not important for `fin.close()`, because the program ends after that anyway. But it is important that `fin.close()` appear before attempting to open `fout`, because otherwise the file remains exclusively attached to the `fin` object and the `fout` would fail.
- Both `print` and `fout.write` are used because there is output to both the console and a file.
- The file output statements skip to the next line after sending their output to the file – is this important? What would happen if they did not skip to the next line?
- This code listing is rather long and complicated. If there were any typing mistakes, what would errors look like? Try making some errors and see for yourself – you could leave out the Python module imports, semicolons, or open statements, etc. Note that some errors get by Python and do not show up until you run the program.

Here's a handy table of interchangeable code blocks for opening a text file for output:

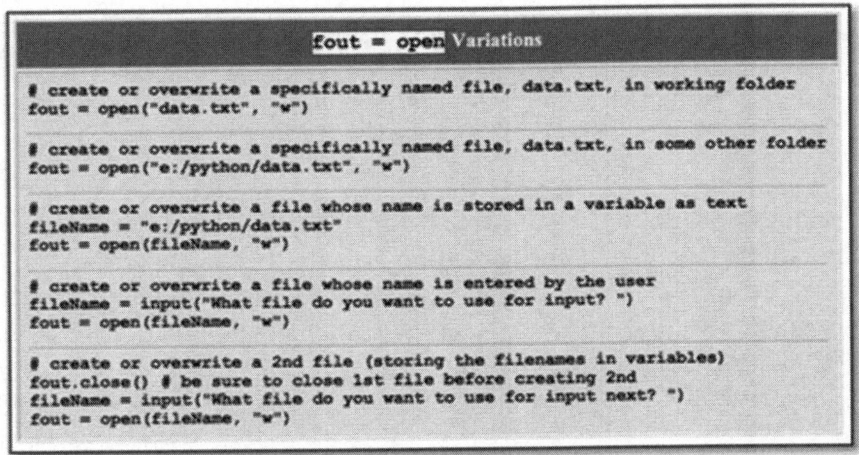

fout = open Variations

```
# create or overwrite a specifically named file, data.txt, in working folder
fout = open("data.txt", "w")

# create or overwrite a specifically named file, data.txt, in some other folder
fout = open("e:/python/data.txt", "w")

# create or overwrite a file whose name is stored in a variable as text
fileName = "e:/python/data.txt"
fout = open(fileName, "w")

# create or overwrite a file whose name is entered by the user
fileName = input("What file do you want to use for input? ")
fout = open(fileName, "w")

# create or overwrite a 2nd file (storing the filenames in variables)
fout.close() # be sure to close 1st file before creating 2nd
fileName = input("What file do you want to use for input next? ")
fout = open(fileName, "w")
```

10.2.2 Appending To A Text File

By default, any existing text file is discarded and overwritten when you open it for output. But it is possible for your program to *append*, or add to an existing file instead of overwriting it. This is useful if you are building a database of transactions, for example, where each new transaction gets saved to a file. Here is how to open an output text file for appending instead of overwriting -- the `"a"` is for "append":

```
fout = open("data.txt", "a")
```

In the above, if the file does not already exist, it is created, as it would have been without the specification to append. Here is an example of using a text file to append output – it is a program that builds a class roster:

Appending Output To A Text File [classRoster.py]

```
# read a student's name from the keyboard (see 5.2.1)
name = input("What is your name? ")

# write the student's name to classRoster.txt
fout = open("classRoster.txt", "a")
fout.write(name + "\n")
fout.close()
```

Note the change in the file open statement that specifies that the output file be appended to, instead of overwritten. Save and run the program, and note that the output file is created the first time you run the program – you do not need to create it in advance! (By the way, this applies to any and all of the `fout = open` code block variations!)

By introducing logic in your programs, they can behave differently depending on circumstances. For example, in the class roster program above, what if the user enters a blank name (by pressing ENTER without typing their name first)? If this is the case, the program should not add the blank name to the text file. Or what if the name is a duplicate of a name already in the **classRoster.txt** file? Again, the program should not add the name. What if the **scores.txt** does not exist when you run the keeping-scores program from the previous chapter? Wouldn't it be better for the program to continue, setting the numbers of wins and losses both to zero, rather than terminating with an error?

Here's an example that modifies the class roster program:

Testing A True-False Condition

```
if len(name) > 0:
   fout = open("classRoster.txt", "a")
   fout.write(name + "\n")
   fout.close()
```

The `>` means “is greater than”. Remember that the `len()` function gets the number of characters stored in text. So this expression tests “if the number of characters stored in the variable `name` is greater than zero, then use the code indented below.”

10.3 Exercises, Sample Code, Videos, And Addendums

Go to www.rdb3.com/python/10 for extended materials pertaining to this chapter.

PART 3 Processing Data

Chapter 11. Checking It Twice: Arrays

An "array" is a variable that can store more than one value *at the same time*. The variables that we have studied up to now can also store more than one value, but only one at a time. Whenever such a variable is set to a new value, the previous value is lost – only the *last* value is ever remembered. But not so for an array – it can remember a sequence of values. What you need to know about arrays is how to declare them, how to copy values into them and retrieve them later, how to "traverse" them, and how to use them with functions.

Consider this problem – we want to get the average of a series of numbers stored in a text file. That's not too hard:

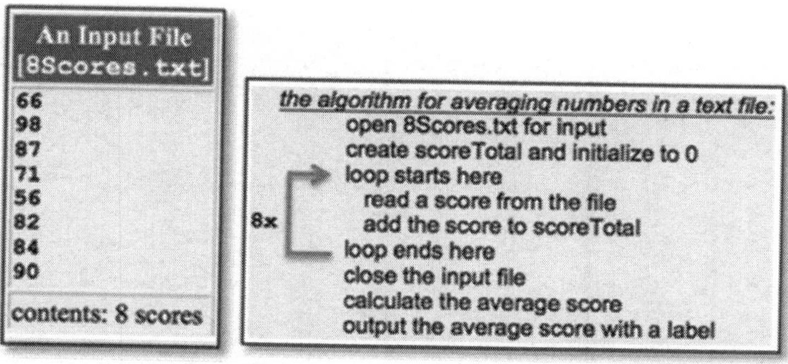

Averaging Numbers In A Text File [avgFile.py]

```
# open 8Scores.txt for input
fileName = "8Scores.txt"
try:
  fin = open(fileName)
except:
  print(fileName, "not found")
  exit() # end the program NOW

# read the scores and build the sum
scoreTotal = 0
for i in range(8):
  aScore = int(fin.readline().strip())
  scoreTotal += aScore
fin.close()

# calculate and output the average
average = scoreTotal / 8
print("The average of 8 numbers is", average)
```

But what if we want to modify the program to count the number of scores that are *greater than the average*? We would have to reopen the file and re-read it, which is possible, but there has to be a better way. (Fortunately the numbers are read from a text file instead of the keyboard – it would be *really* hard to ask a user to re-enter all of the data!)

The solution is to *store each individual value* as it is read from the file (or from the keyboard) in the memory of the computer. Then we can access them again and again, as often as we wish, without going back to the original source of the data. For this, computer languages have array variables.

11.1 Array Variables

An array is a variable that can hold more than one value by the same name. It uses an "index" to distinguish among the many values stored in it. Here's how to create an array variable – an "array" for short – showing its conceptual representation:

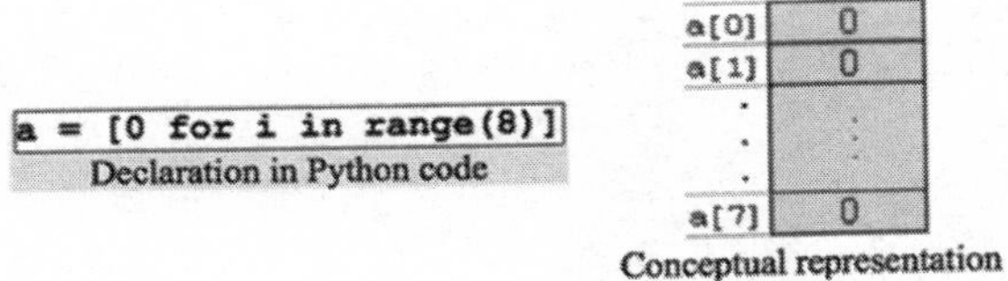

Declaration in Python code

Conceptual representation

This variable **a** can store 8 values at the same time! The first value is referenced as a[0] and the last as a[7], using "square brackets" around the index number. You say these as "a of zero" and "a of seven". Each of these is called an "element" of the array. They are used like any other variable containing a whole number, for example:

```
a[0] = 100;
a[1] = 17;
.
.
.
a[7] = -99;
```

a[0]	100
a[1]	17
.	
.	
.	
a[7]	-99

Representation in code Conceptual representation

The array index value can be expressed not only as a value, but also as a variable (or an expression that results in a whole number). This means it can be used in a count-controlled loop, using the loop counter as an index. It's as if arrays and for-loops were made for each other!

Before we look at some details, let's consider this solution to the averaging problem posed above:

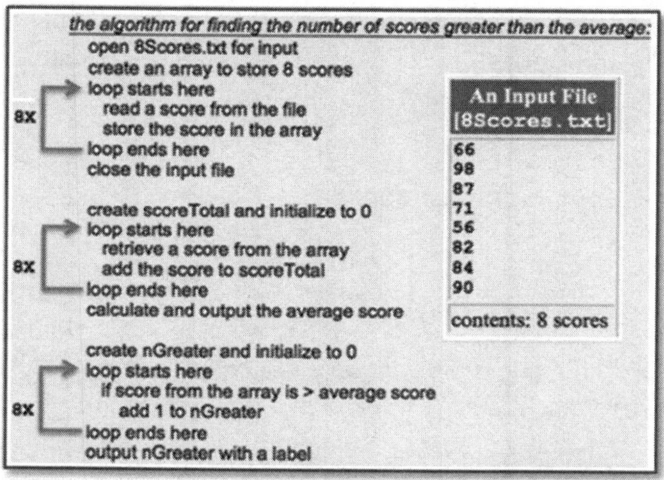

Finding The Number Of Scores Greater Than The Average [avgFile2.py]

```
# open 8Scores.txt for input
fileName = "8Scores.txt"
try:
  fin = open(fileName)
except:
  print(fileName, "not found")
  exit() # end the program NOW

# read and save the scores
score = [0 for i in range(8)]
for i in range(8):
  score[i] = int(fin.readline().strip())
fin.close()

# calculate and output the average
scoreTotal = 0
for i in range(8):
  scoreTotal += score[i]
average = scoreTotal / 8
print("The average of 8 numbers is", average)

# count #of scores > average
nGreater = 0
for i in range(8):
  if score[i] > average:
    nGreater += 1
print(nGreater, "scores are greater than the average.")
```

There's a lot going on here, so let's take a look.

There are three successive loops in this program. Each is its own code block, separated by blank lines and headed by a comment line. The first loop simply reads the values from the file and stores them.

The second loop totals the elements of the array. Actually, the first and second loops could have been combined and done as one loop! The third loop runs through the saved scores and compares each to the average, counting those greater.

Also note that the number 8 appears throughout this program, and it's not good programming practice

11.1.1 Array Size

The "array size" is the number of elements in the array. In our examples, the size of the array named `score` is 8 – that's what the `8` is for in `[0 for i in range(8)]`. When a Python array is created, the values initially stored in those 8 elements are whole number zeros – that's what the `0` is for in `[0 for i in range(8)]`.

Also note that the number 8 appears throughout this program, and it's not good programming practice to repeat a value. It's better to save it in a variable and just use that variable instead. Actually, Python has better way to blend for-loops and arrays as we'll soon see, that avoids the issue altogether!

11.1.2 Array Traversal

The use of a for-loop to process each element of an array is called "traversal". This is the powerful thing about using arrays. Arrays let us store large numbers of values easily, and for-loops let us process them easily.

Here's how you would traverse an array and set all of its elements to zero – of course, they start out as zero in Python, but you can set them to any other value as well:

Traversing An Array To Set Its Values To Zero

```
a = [0 for i in range(8)]

for i in range(len(a)):
  a[i] = 0
```

Note that the size of the Python array named "a" is retrieved as `len(a)`. Python arrays track their size.

Here's how you would traverse an array and set all of its elements via the keyboard:

Traversing An Array To Set Values Via The Keyboard

```
a = [0 for i in range(8)]

for i in range(len(a)):
  print("Please enter a[", i, "] = ", sep="", end="")
  a[i] = int(input())
```

Here's how you would traverse an array and send its values to the console for output:

Traversing An Array To Output Its Values

```
for i in range(len(a)):
  print("a[", i, "] =", a[i])
```

11.1.3 List Comprehension

When Python arrays are created, the values of their elements can all be zeroed out. But it is possible to specify the values of each element upon declaration. It's called "list comprehension" and it is done like this:

```
daysPerMonth = [31, 28, 31, 30, 31, 30, 31, 31, 30, 31, 30, 31]
```

Note that the array size is not specified in the square brackets. Instead, the computer *counts* the number of elements and makes the array exactly that size.

11.2 Array Processing

Arrays are processed by traversal. In traversal, you access each element of the array, one-by-one, for assignment, output, or any other operation. Some more advanced types of array processing involve searching and sorting.

11.2.1 Searching An Array

The **avgFile2.py** program from earlier in this chapter actually contains examples of searching. The last loop traverses the array, looking for values greater than the average, and counts them. It provides a good model for searching, and can be applied to any number of situations. Here is that loop:

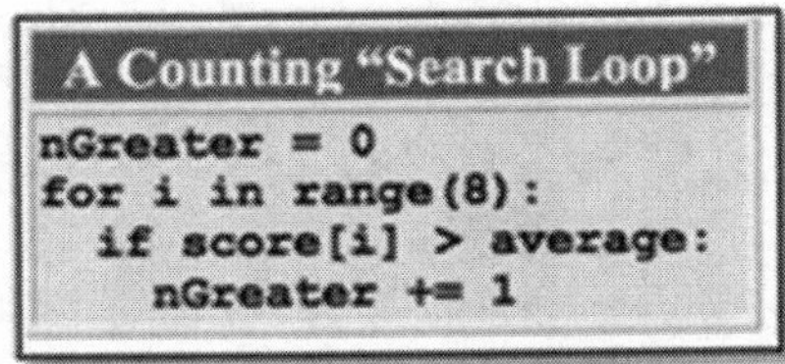

A Counting "Search Loop"
nGreater = 0
for i in range(8):
  if score[i] > average:
    nGreater += 1

Here is what you should notice about this "search loop" – these are things common to all search loops: First, a variable is declared above the loop, which stores the piece of information we want from the search. But it is set to the wrong value (presumably): zero! It looks like we know the answer in advance, wrongly so, by saying that it is zero. But it is actually just a starting point – it is zero *before* we start our search and until we find otherwise. In other words, until we look at the array's elements, let's just *assume* that the answer is zero. If we find this to be incorrect, we can reset it later.

Next, we traverse the array. Inside the for-loop's code block, there is a test of a single element to see if it matches our search criterion. If it does, we adjust the variable that is *now* seen to have been incorrectly set to zero. We continue to adjust this variable's value as we inspect and test each element. When the loop completes, the variable now contains the correct value.

The variable `nGreater` is called an "accumulator". It is a variable that gets set to an assumed value *before* the search loop starts, and gets adjusted inside the loop. `scoreTotal` in the same example is also an accumulator – it is assumed to be zero, and adjusted as each element is inspected.

Here is another example that finds whether or not there are any perfect scores:

A Boolean Search Loop

```
hasPerfectScore = False
for i in range(len(score)):
  if score[i] == 100:
    hasPerfectScore = True
    break
```

It starts out with an accumulator named `hasPerfectScore`, which we assume to be false (until proven to be true). The code block breaks out of the loop once a perfect score is found – there is no point in looking any further!

11.2.2 Finding A Maximum Or Minimum Value

We can now complete the classic solution introduced in chapters 6, 7, and 8 – the one that finds the maximum or minimum value in a set of values. Here are some code blocks that show how this is done:

Finding The Maximum Or Minimum Value

```
# find the maximum
maximum = score[0]
for i in range(1, len(score)):
  if maximum < score[i]: maximum = score[i]
```

```
# find the minimum
minimum = score[0]
for i in range(1, len(score)):
  if minimum > score[i]: minimum = score[i]
```

```
# find maximum AND minimum
maximum = score[0]
minimum = score[0]
for i in range(1, len(score)):
  if maximum < score[i]: maximum = score[i]
  if minimum > score[i]: minimum = score[i]
```

Note that the accumulators are initialized to the first element of the array. That is because until we look beyond the first element, as far as we know, it is the maximum *and* the minimum – the *only* value. The for-loop starts with element one instead of zero – that's because there is no point in comparing the first element to itself. It's done by putting `1,` inside the `range` specification, telling the loop start with `i` equal to 1 instead of the usual 0. It would not hurt to start at 0 instead of 1, though.

11.2.3 Sorting An Array With A Code Block

We can also complete the other classic solution introduced in chapters 6 and 8 – the one that *rearranges* the elements of an array so that they are in numerical order, low-to-high or high-to-low. The same applies to an array of text values, which may be arranged in alphabetical order, or perhaps in the order of the shortest to the longest text. You can sort arrays using a code block, or using a module function. Both ways are shown here. For variety, these examples use arrays of text.

Sorting Text In Alphabetical Order [textSort.py]

```
# create an array with the days of the week
day = ["Monday", "Tuesday", "Wednesday", \
    "Thursday", "Friday", "Saturday", "Sunday"]

# output contents of the array, in original order
print("Unsorted: ", end = "")
for i in range(len(day)):
  print(day[i], end = " ")
print()

# 2 nested for-loops to sort the array
for i in range(len(day)):
  for j in range(i + 1, len(day)):
    if day[i] > day[j]:
      day[i],day[j] = day[j],day[i]

# output contents, in alphabetical order
print("Sorted: ", end = "")
for i in range(len(day)):
  print(day[i], end = " ")
print()
```

Let's look at this sorting example more closely. First, the array contains 7 text values, initialized to the days of the week in chronological order. Next, there is a loop that traverses and outputs the array elements before they are sorted. Then there is a code block that uses *nested for-loops* – one inside the code block of another. Since `i` is already being used as a counter in the first (or *outer*) loop, we cannot use it again in the second (or *inner*) loop without creating lots of confusion! So a new counter, `j`, is introduced. The two loops work together to compare two elements of the array, and swap them if they are out of order with respect to one another.

Note that the inner loop starts `j` with the value `i + 1` instead of zero. This is a critical feature of the sorting code block, and without this it would not work correctly.

The nested loops sort the text alphabetically, because of the statement `if day[i] > day[j]:`. To sort in reverse alphabetical order, use `<` instead of `>`. In comparing text, remember that case matters. In the ASCII sequence, uppercase letters come before lowercase. So the word "Zebra" actually comes *before* "aardvark", since `'Z'` is ASCII code 90, and `'a'` is code 97. To make a case independent comparison, you would compare `day[i].lower()` to `day[j].lower()` instead (or upper to upper).

You could also compare based on text length instead of alphabetically. To do so, you would change the if-statement like this: `if len(day[i]) > len(day[j]):`. If you did this for our particular case, note that there are several "ties" – 4 days have 6 letters in their names. Since we do not include in the if-statement how to handle ties, it's left to the computer to decide.

For sorting an array of numbers low-to-high, the if-statement would be exactly the same as in the sample program, **textSort.py**.

11.2.4 Sorting An Array With A Function Call

The Python function `sort` sorts an array with one statement – no nested for-loops are required! Here's an example. For variety, the data is read from a file – the same text file from the start of this chapter.

Sorting An Array Of Numbers [sortFile.py]

```
# open 8Scores.txt for input
fileName = "8Scores.txt"
try:
  fin = open(fileName)
except:
  print(fileName, "not found")
  exit() # end the program NOW

# read and save the scores
score = [0 for i in range(8)]
for i in range(len(score)):
  score[i] = int(fin.readline().strip())
fin.close()

score.sort()

# output the sorted scores
for i in range(len(score)):
  print(score[i], end = " ")
print()
```

11.3 Dynamically-Sized Arrays

When we created the arrays earlier in this chapter, all were created with a specific size known by the programmer before the program was saved to its file. The size of 8 for the array of scores read from the text file **8Scores.txt** had to match the number of scores in the file, or there would be a problem. It would be nice if the *first* line of the file could tell the program how many elements to have in its array.

Python allows the number of elements to be specified by a *variable*. Here is the statement to declare an array of `n` elements, where `n` is a variable:

```
score = [0 for i in range(n)]
```

Python allows the number inside the square brackets of an array declaration to be either a literal whole number or a variable containing a whole number. So the problem of the 8-element array easily goes away by adding a count to the text file, reading it into a variable, and using that variable to declare the array instead of the number 8:

Using A Dynamic Array [dynamicArray.py]

```
# open scores.txt for input
fileName = "score.txt"
try:
  fin = open(fileName)
  size = int(fin.readline().strip())
except:
  print(fileName, "not found")
  exit() # end the program NOW

# read and save the scores
score = [0 for i in range(size)]
for i in range(size):
  score[i] = int(fin.readline().strip())
fin.close()

# output the scores to the console
for i in range(size):
  print(score[i], end = " ")
print()
```

An Input File [score.txt]

```
8
66
98
87
71
56
82
84
90
```

Note that after the file is opened, the number "8" is transferred from the first line of the file into the variable `size`, which is used to specify the array size.

Actually, any non-negative integer value can be used to create a dynamically sized array, including zero. Yes, it is possible to have an array of size zero in Python! It may not seem like that would ever be useful, but it can be, although we will not consider such cases in this book.

11.3.1 Multiple Values From A Single Line Of Input

In chapters 5 and 10, we showed how to capture values entered from the keyboard or read from a text file. But we could only enter one value at a time (that is, each followed by the ENTER key), or have one value per line in the text file. Using dynamic arrays, it is possible to read an array of values from a single line of input! Here are some code examples, using both console and file input:

Getting Multiple Values From A Single Line Of Input
Reading An Array Of Values With Python

```
a = input().split() # console

a = fin.readline().strip().split() # file

# now "a" is an array of size len(a)!
```

In these examples, the values are separated by a *single space*, as specified between the square brackets of the `split` call. For tab-separated values, use `.split("\t")`, and for comma-separated use `.split(",")`.

11.4 Arrays In Function Parameter Lists

Array variables can be shared with functions by using the parameter list, much like other variables. But before we see how this is done, there is one major difference that programmers need to be aware of. When regular variables are shared with functions, *copies* are made. So if the copy gets changed in the function, it does not affect the original. This is called "pass by value".

But when an *array* is shared with a function, no copies are made – instead, the *original* array is shared. Any changes made to the elements of the array inside the function *do* affect the original array! This is called "pass by reference".

There's no special way to specify an array in the parameter list – it's just like any other variable. In the following example, an array is shared with a function whose job is to return the average of the elements in the array:

An Averaging Function

```
def getAverage(score):
  result = 0
  total = 0
  for i in range(len(score)):
    total += score[i]
  result = total / len(score)
  return result
# getAverage ends here

# main program starts here
...
score = [0 for i in range(...)]
print("Average = ", getAverage(score))
...
```

Try adding this code to any of the preceding programs that have a `score` array, tracking the array size as `len(score)`. Note that the array name is the same in the main program and in the function – this is by programmer choice and it is *not* a requirement. Even though they both refer to the exact same array, it's okay to have different names, or *aliases*, for the same array in different scopes.

11.5 Arrays And Functions Together

To show how arrays and functions work together, let's rewrite **avgFile2.py** with functions. One of the functions will be used to read the file, fill the array, and send the array back to the main program. In so doing, the details of getting values for the array are left to a *function*, as are the details of averaging the values and sending them to the console screen as output.

Arrays And Functions Together [avgFile3.py]

```
def readScores(score):
  # open 8Scores.txt for input
  fileName = "8Scores.txt"
  try:
    fin = open(fileName)
  except:
    print(fileName, "not found")
    return # end the function NOW

  # read and save the scores
  for i in range(len(score)):
    score[i] = int(fin.readline().strip())
  fin.close()
# readScores ends here

def getAverage(score):
  # calculate and output the average
  result = 0
  scoreTotal = 0
  for i in range(len(score)):
    scoreTotal += score[i]
  result = scoreTotal / len(score)
  return result
# getAverage ends here

def countScoresGreaterThan(score, x):
  # count #of scores > average
  result = 0
  for i in range(len(score)):
    if score[i] > average:
      result += 1
  return result
# countScoresGreaterThan ends here

# main program starts here
score = [0 for i in range(8)]
readScores(score)
average = getAverage(score)
print("The average is", average)
print(countScoresGreaterThan(score, average), \
  "scores are greater than the average.")
```

The above example contains several "design considerations", or programmer choices, which could have been done any number of ways. Let's discuss why things are done the way they are in the example code:

11.5.1 Bailing Out Of A Function Early

There is a `return` statement in the void function `readScores` instead of `exit()`. It's not really necessary to have made this change, but it just shows that you can exit a function early without having to end the program. Program execution continues after the call to `readScores` with all the original zeros for the scores.

11.5.2 Local Variables In Functions

The `result` variables that are declared inside the value-returning functions are called "local variables", because they each belong to their own function. They are in separate scopes, and are therefore, separate and distinct variables. They only exist while the program is executing the code in their function.

`fin` and `scoreTotal` are also local variables, privately owned by their functions.

11.5.3 Parameter List Variable Names

The second parameter in `countScoresGreater` is named `x` in the parameter list, but the call in the main program has a variable named `average` in that position. The names do not match, and they do not have to. Whether the names refer to separate copies values from the main program, or they are aliases for arrays in the main program, the *names* are local to their functions. In the same way, a person can go by two different names – one at work and another at home – array variables can, too. Array variables have *aliases* across function scopes.

The reason for using a generic name like `x` in the function is to make `countScoresGreater` more generic. There is really no reason that it cannot be used to count the number of scores greater than *any* value – not just the average. By writing it as generic as possible, it is available to be used for other things, such as counting the number of A's (scores greater than 89).

11.5.4 Temporary Variables

The variable `average` in the main program is used to store the result of the `getAverage` call. It is really not needed, though, because `average` could be replaced where it appears in the two output statements with `getAverage(score)`. But doing so would require that the averaging loop be executed twice, which is a bit of a waste. So programmers generally will use an extra "temporary variable" to store the result of a call that is used multiple times.

Note that this was not done with `countScoresGreater`, because it is only called once.

11.5.5 Pass By Reference

In `readScores`, array elements are assigned values. Since arrays are *passed by reference*, the function gets the *original* version of the array, and any changes made to it affect the main program where the array was declared. This would not be so for anything that is not an array – they are *passed by value*, meaning that the function has a *copy* of the original value. Any change made to a copy in the function does not affect the original in the main program.

11.5.6 Array As A Return Type

It's okay to create a Python array and return it from a function. Here's how that could be done in the previous sample program:

Returning An Array

```
def readScores():
  result = [] # a zero-length array
  # open 8Scores.txt for input
  fileName = "8Scores.txt"
  try:
    fin = open(fileName)
    result = [0 for i in range(8)]
  except:
    print(fileName, "not found")
    return result # end the function NOW

  # read and save the scores
  for i in range(len(result)):
    result[i] = int(fin.readline().strip())
  fin.close()
  return result
# readScores ends here

# main program starts here
...
score = readScores()
```

11.6 Exercises, Sample Code, Videos, And Addendums

Go to www.rdb3.com/python/11 for extended materials pertaining to this chapter.

Chapter 12. Using Objects

Like the array, an "object" is a variable that can store multiple values at the same time. But the values stored in arrays are usually all the same thing, like all scores or all temperatures or all names. An object can store all the values associated with, for example, a student's school record, like their name as text, their ID as a whole number, and their grade-point-average as a floating point – all in one variable called an *object*.

Actually, the Python array *is* an object, too, but it's got that special restriction about all values being the same thing, so array objects get a special syntax (square-bracket indexing) that takes advantage of that. Other objects don't get to use the square-bracket syntax. They use the dot syntax, like a file object's `.close()`, as we'll soon see.

Objects can be visualized as database records, which may have multiple data items, or "fields", such as name, address, city, state, and zip code. Such data does not lend itself very well to single-value variables, because you'd have to use a separate variable for each field. That's fine, but what if you are working with multiple records? Now you need arrays for each field, and you have to manage each one. If you want to use functions, you have to list each field separately in the parameter list, and if you ever add *more* fields, you have to change *all* the parameter lists.

12.1 Object Specifications

The first thing you have to do in order to use objects is to decide on what fields you want. For our example, let's consider a student's school record as an object, with fields for name, student ID, and grade point average. We could add a lot more to this, but let's keep it simple for the sake of learning.

Each field needs a "field name". These have to be valid Python identifiers, like variable names and function names. Let's use `name`, `id`, and `gpa`. Also, the whole structure needs an identifier – let's use **`Student`**. Here is how all of this gets put together in code, and what it represents conceptually:

```
class Student:
  name = None
  id = None
  gpa = None
# Student specification ends here
```

Representation in Python code

table: Student		
name	id	gpa

Conceptual representation

`None` means that when an object is created, it's created without a name, student ID, and grade point average – these are to be assigned *after* the object's creation.

Conceptually, an "object specification" represents an empty data table, with each row able to represent one record, and each column representing a field. Note that just specifying an object is like typing column headings – rows containing values will be added later, as the table starts out empty.

The object specification appears inside its own indented code block, headed by the **`class`** keyword. It goes *below* any **`import`** statement(s), and *above* any functions.

You can use any previously defined class for a field in your object specification – even one defined by yourself, as long as it's specification appears above.

12.2 Objects

The whole idea of writing a specification for an object is so there can be single variables and arrays of variables that can hold all of the data fields for each object individually. Once specified, you can use your new class in the same way you use numbers and text, except for assignment and retrieval of field values, which is a new thing. So you can declare them, specify them as returns from value-returning functions, include them in parameter lists, and make arrays of them.

12.2.1 Object Declarations

Here are declaration statements that can go in any code block, and a conceptual picture of initially empty records being added to the data table:

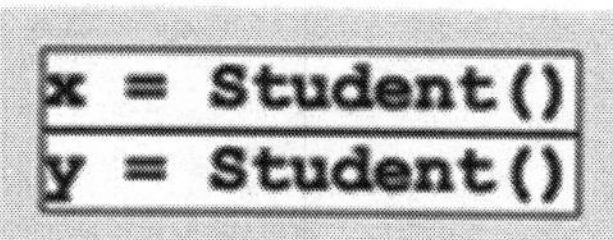

table: Student

	name	id	gpa
x	None	None	None
y	None	None	None

This is exactly how other objects are declared, like `fin` and `fout`, except that there's nothing inside the parentheses for our `Student` objects.

12.2.2 Using Object Data Fields

But there are some things you cannot do with objects, such as use one directly in a `print` statement. The computer does *not* know to format an object and represent it in output.

The Python language provides the "dot operator" to get to a specific field by its identifier. For example, for a `Student` object stored in a variable named `a`, the way to get to the name of the student is `a.name`. Likewise, the remaining fields are `a.id` and `a.gpa`. Each of these behaves exactly like the data type that it is, so to get the length of student `a`'s name, use `len(a.name)`. To set `a`'s grade point average, use for example `a.gpa = 3.67`.

```
# creating two objects
a = Student()
b = Student()
```

```
a.name = "George"
a.id = 17890
a.gpa = 3.67
```

```
b.name = "John"
b.id = 17970
b.gpa = 3.53
```

table: Student

	name	id	gpa
a	George	17890	3.67
b	John	17970	3.53

Field values can also be read directly from a text file. To read object **a**'s ID from a file, use:

```
# reading data into an object
a.id = int(fin.readline().strip())
```

To show object **a** on the console screen, do something like this:

```
# sending object fields to the console screen
print("Name=", a.name, end = "")
print(", ID=", a.id, end = "")
print(", GPA=", a.gpa)
```

You might think that `x = y` assigns (or copies) all of the fields of **y** to **x** (as it does in C++), so that they are both separate copies of the same object, but in Python (as in Java), it *makes* **x** *an alias for* **y**, and thereby totally loses track of the student formerly known as **x**!

12.3 Arrays Of Objects

Conceptually, an array of objects is like a spreadsheet table, with each row representing *one* object. With such an array in memory, you can do all kinds of things, including searching and sorting – anything you can do using a traversing for-loop. The code for an object array is a straightforward application of everything we already know. For example:

```
a = [Student() for i in range(30)]
```

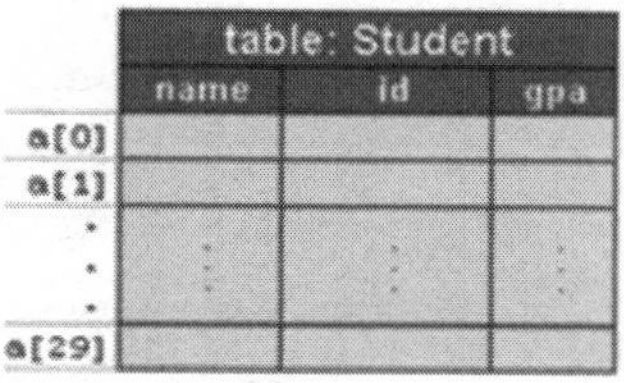

	name	id	gpa
a[0]			
a[1]			
.	:	:	:
a[29]			

table: Student

The way to get to the name of the first student object is `a[0].name`. The remaining fields are `a[0].id` and `a[0].gpa`. The length of the first student's name is `len(a[0].name)`, which looks complicated, but is not so bad when you break it down into parts. To set the grade point average of the first student, use e.g., `a[0].gpa = 3.67`. To read the first student's ID from a text file, use:

```
# reading arrayed object's data from a file
a[0].id = int(fin.readline().strip())
```

12.4 Objects And Functions

Objects can be used in functions just like any other variable. They can be returned by value-returning functions, they can be parameters, and they can be local variables.

12.4.1 Returning An Object From A Value-Returning Function

This example uses the standard value-returning function 3-step structure, declaring a variable, setting its value, and returning it. It's returned value gets stored in `s` in the main program:

Objects In Value-Returning Functions

```
def getGeorge():
  result = Student() # step 1
  ...
  return result # step 3
# getGeorge ends here
```

```
# main program starts here
s = getGeorge()
```

12.4.2 An Object As A Function Parameter

The following example adds a void function with an object as its parameter – note that it works just like any other parameter, except that they are passed by reference, just like arrays, so `x` in the function is an *alias* for `s` in main – they both refer to the same object.

Objects As Function Parameters

```
def outputRecord(x):
  print(x.name)
  ...
#outputRecord ends here
```

```
# main program starts here
...
s = Student()
...
outputRecord(s);
...
```

The main reason for doing this is that objects can be large, and for memory and efficiency reasons, it is better to avoid making copies. Another reason is so that any changes made to the fields of the object in the function affect the variable in the main program, because it is an *alias* for the original object. Arrays and objects work this way by default. The following example has an object with three fields representing the time-of-day. It has a void function to output a `tod` object in a nicely formatted way.

Time Objects [todTest.py]

```
class tod:
  hour = None
  minute = None
  second = None
# tod specification ends here

def outputTod(t):
  print("{:02}".format(t.hour), end=":")
  print("{:02}".format(t.minute), end=":")
  print("{:02}".format(t.second))
# outputTod ends here

#main program starts here
noon = tod()
noon.hour = 12
noon.minute = 0
noon.second = 0
outputTod(noon)
```

12.5 Object-Oriented Programming

There's actually a lot more to objects than has been covered in this book. In fact, "object-oriented programming" is a subject worthy of a full semester course in itself.

We've created our own objects by specifying data fields. But what about `fin` and `fout` that we call objects? There certainly seems to be a lot more to those objects than our `Student` and `tod`. It turns out that you can define custom *behaviors* for objects, like `fin.readline()` – that tells the object to read a line from its associated file.

We won't deal with behaviors in this book, except to use behaviors defined for objects that are already in Python. Defining our own behaviors is a topic left for future study.

12.6 Exercises, Sample Code, Videos, And Addendums

Go to www.rdb3.com/python/12 for extended materials pertaining to this chapter.

Chapter 13. Keeping A List: Array-Based Lists

What you need to know about array-based lists is that they are arrays in which not all of the elements are used, but are available for use in case they are needed. A new, separate variable is used to track how many of the elements are actually in use at any time. Unlike previous chapters, the purpose of this chapter is *not* to train you in the use of this programming feature. It is instead an opportunity to introduce concepts that you will run into if you go further in your study of computer science, and to provide a way to practice the programming features we studied in preceding chapters.

A "list" is a collection of values – usually objects, but they can be whole numbers or floating points or text, too. The Python language allows the data types for these to be different from one another, even in the same collection! This concept is that of a "bag", which can contain lots of different items. But for purposes of our study in this book, we will consider collections of *like* data only.

A list can be "empty" – that is, it can have zero values stored in it. Lists can grow in size by adding values, and shrink by taking them away. By contrast, the arrays that we studied in chapter 11 were of fixed, non-zero size, and each element had a value, even if it was zero. So there are similarities and differences between arrays and lists. For example, with an array or a list, we could store test scores. But with a list we could find the lowest test score and remove it, or add a new score for a late assignment.

There are several ways to represent lists in computers, and we will study these in this and the remaining chapters of this book. One way is to use arrays, and that's the subject of this chapter.

13.1 Array-Based Lists

Arrays are sized when they are created, and we normally consider all of their elements to be assigned valid values. An "array-based list" takes the idea of an array, but considers that the elements may not all be in use. The elements are placeholders for values that may or may not ever be assigned. The list's underlying array is divided into two parts – the front part, which has elements with assigned values, and the back part, which has elements in reserve for possible future use. To mark the dividing point, a variable is used to track the number of elements that have valid, assigned values. It looks something like the figure below.

nNames	3
name[0]	George
name[1]	John
name[2]	Thomas
name[3]	*unused*
. . .	⋮
name[98]	*unused*
name[99]	*unused*

Conceptual representation

The variable `nNames` is the "list size". It not only tracks the number of elements in use at the time, but it also serves as a dividing line between valid, assigned elements, and as-yet unassigned. In the example, 3 elements are in use, the rest not (yet).

The following example code blocks show what you need in order to declare array-based lists of various kinds, all initially empty. Note the naming convention used – the array names are not plural, so that `student[0]` is the first student object. The name of the list size variable is the same as that of the array, but plural, with a leading "n", and the first letter uppercased. The "list capacity" is named "MAX_" plus the uppercase, plural name of the array – it's the *array size* of the list's array.

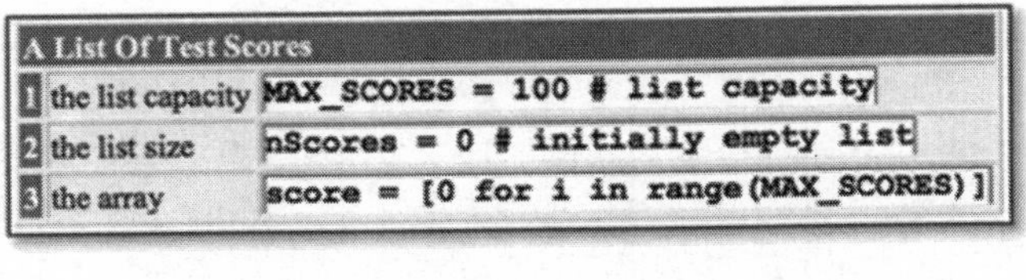

A List Of Test Scores		
1	the list capacity	`MAX_SCORES = 100 # list capacity`
2	the list size	`nScores = 0 # initially empty list`
3	the array	`score = [0 for i in range(MAX_SCORES)]`

A List Of Names		
1	the list capacity	`MAX_NAMES = 20 # list capacity`
2	the list size	`nNames = 0 # initially empty list`
3	the array	`name = ["" for i in range(MAX_NAMES)]`

A List Of Student Objects		
1	the list capacity	`MAX_STUDENTS = 30 # list capacity`
2	the list size	`nStudents = 0 # initially empty list`
3	the array	`student = [Student() for i in range(MAX_STUDENTS)]`

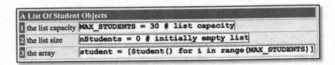

13.1.1 Adding Values To A List

By default, new values are added at the end of the list. Here is the code for adding values to the ends of the lists created above, as long as the list capacity is not exceeded:

Adding Values To A List

```
aScore = ... # value to be added
if nScores < MAX_SCORES:
  score[nScores] = aScore
  nScores += 1

aName = ... # value to be added
 if (nNames < MAX_NAMES)
  name[nNames] = aName
  nNames += 1

aStudent = Student()
aStudent.name = ...
... # assign other fields
if (nStudents < MAX_STUDENTS)
  student[nStudents] = aStudent
  nStudents += 1
```

In the previous chapters, we loaded values directly into the array. But it's different with lists. We first store a new value in a temporary variable, like `aScore`, which stands for "a score". Then we check to see if the list is not full, and if it's not full, we copy the temporary variable's value into the next available position in the array.

The following is a rewrite of an earlier example from chapter 11, but in this example the number of scores in the input file is *not* known in advance, and not stored in the input file's first line. Using a list, there is really no need to know the number of scores in the file in advance, and the program is protected against the possibility of there being too many scores to handle (that is, more than 100).

Reading An Unknown Number Of Values Into A List [listFile.py]

```
try:
  fin = open("many.txt")
except:
  print("file not found")
  exit() # end the program NOW

# create the list
MAX_SCORES = 100
nScores = 0
score = [0 for i in range(MAX_SCORES)]

# read and save the scores
for lineFromFile in fin:
  aScore = int(lineFromFile.strip()) # read a score from the file
  if nScores < MAX_SCORES:  # if list is not full...
    score[nScores] = aScore # ...add new score to list
    nScores += 1
fin.close()

# find the average
scoreTotal = 0
for i in range(nScores):
  scoreTotal += score[i]
average = scoreTotal / nScores
print("The average of", nScores, "numbers is", average)

# count number of scores > average
nGreater = 0
for i in range(nScores):
  if score[i] > average: nGreater += 1
print(nGreater, "scores are greater than the average.")
```

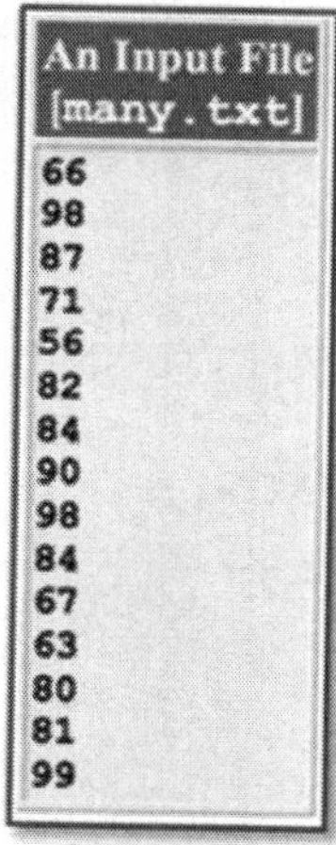

An Input File [many.txt]

```
66
98
87
71
56
82
84
90
98
84
67
63
80
81
99
```

Note that the first loop reads values from the file, until the end of the file is reached. The if-statement inside the loop protects against overfilling the array that supports the list. There is no error message in this example, in case the list capacity is exceeded – new values are simply read and ignored. But it would not be difficult to add code to either output a message or set a Boolean flag, as modeled in section 9.4.

13.1.2 Searching And Sorting A List

With array-based lists, the code for searching and sorting is almost the same as it was for the arrays we studied in chapter 11. The difference is that the *list size* is used for the end of count-controlled traversal loops instead of the *array size* (which is the same as the *list capacity*). So the counting search loop that counts the number of values greater than the average becomes this:

Similarly, the Boolean search loop becomes this, even if `nScores` is zero:

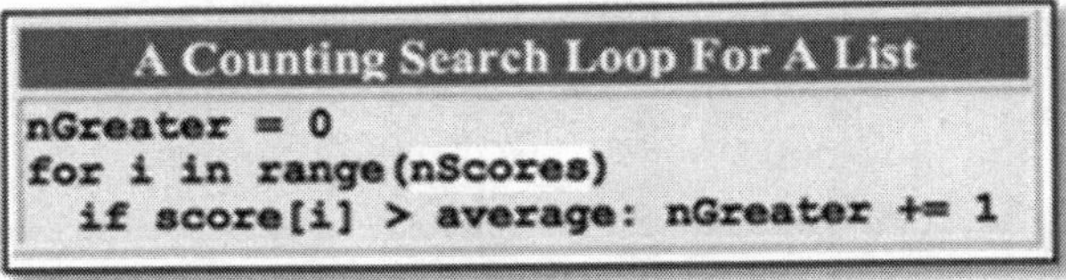

A Counting Search Loop For A List

```
nGreater = 0
for i in range(nScores)
  if score[i] > average: nGreater += 1
```

A Boolean Search Loop For A List

```
hasPerfectScore = False
for i in range(nScores):
  if score[i] == 100:
    hasPerfectScore = True
    break
```

And for values of `nScores` other than zero, the value range search loops become:

Finding The Maximum Or Minimum Value Of A List

```
# find the maximum
maximum = score[0]
for i in range(1, nScores):
  if maximum < score[i]: maximum = score[i]
```

```
# find the minimum
minimum = score[0]
for i in range(1, nScores):
  if minimum > score[i]: minimum = score[i]
```

```
# find maximum AND minimum
maximum = score[0]
minimum = score[0]
for i in range(1, nScores):
  if maximum < score[i]: maximum = score[i]
  if minimum > score[i]: minimum = score[i]
```

To sort an array-based list, the sort function call is nearly the same as for a full array. There is just one change, since the sorting does not involve the whole array: it's the size counter inside square brackets, preceded by a colon -- `[:nScores]`. This tells the sort subprogram to sort only the first `nScores` values in the array, and to ignore everything after that.

Sorting A List Of Whole Numbers [sortFileList.py]

```
try:
  fin = open("many.txt")
except:
  print("file not found")
  exit() # end the program NOW

# create the list
MAX_SCORES = 100
nScores = 0
score = [0 for i in range(MAX_SCORES)]

# read and save the scores
for lineFromFile in fin:
  aScore = int(lineFromFile.strip()) # read a score from the file
  if nScores < MAX_SCORES:  # if list is not full...
    score[nScores] = aScore # ...add new score to list
    nScores += 1
fin.close()

score[:nScores].sort() # sort first nScores elements of the array

# output scores in lo-to-hi order
for i in range(nScores):
  print(score[i], end = " ")
print()
```

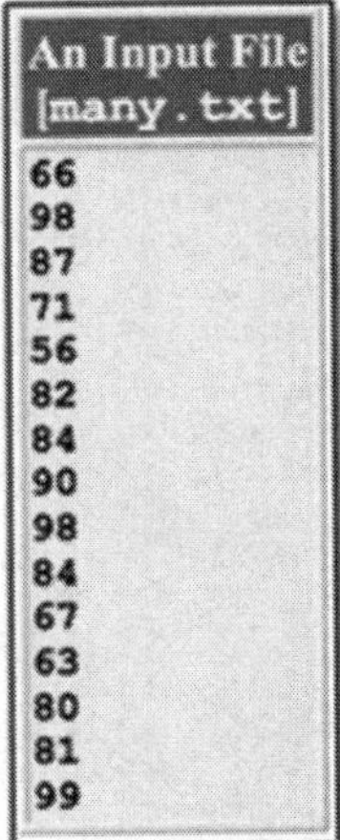

An Input File
[many.txt]

```
66
98
87
71
56
82
84
90
98
84
67
63
80
81
99
```

13.1.3 Function And Array-Based Lists

When sharing an array-based list with a function, remember that there are now *two* values that identify the list – the array and the list size. So any function that receives the array in its parameter list also needs the list size. Here is an example:

An Averaging Function

```
def getAverage(score, n):
  result = 0
  for i in range(n):
    result += score[i];
  result = result / n
  return result
# getAverage ends here

# main program starts here
...
print("Average =", getAverage(score, nScores))
```

Note that the list size is shared with the function *by value*, meaning that the version in the function code block is a *copy*. So if you change it there, it will not affect the *real* size of the list.

13.1.4 Adding And Removing Values

While it is certainly possible to write code for adding values at positions in the list other than at the end, and to remove values at any position, array-based lists do not really lend themselves very well to these operations. The problem is that such operations require mass movement of elements to create/close "gaps" in an array. There are better ways to represent lists, if you need features such as these.

But it is actually not hard to remove the *last* value in an array-based list – the index for its value is the list size minus one (for example, `score[nScores - 1]`). Then you would have to subtract one from the list size (using `nScores -= 1`). Here is the code for removing the a value from the end of a list:

Removing The Last-Added Value

```
if nScores > 0:
  aScore = score[nScores - 1]
  nScores -= 1
  # do something with the removed score
```

```
if nNames > 0
  aName = name[nNames - 1] :
  nNames -= 1
  # do something with the removed name
```

```
if nStudents > 0:
  aStudent = student[nStudents - 1]
  nStudents -= 1
  # do something with the removed object
```

In each of the above examples, a value is removed from the list (even though its "ghost" actually remains in the array!), and is copied to a new, temporary variable (like `aScore`) for further processing in the remainder of the if-statement code block (represented by "...").

13.2 Other Ways To Make Lists

Besides array-based lists, there are "linked lists" which do not use arrays at all, and there are module-based collection objects, which do most of the coding for you and provide a wide range of features. We study the code for linked lists in the next chapter, and collections in the chapter after that.

13.3 An Array-Based List Example

Here is an example of a list of student records, using the `class Student` from chapter 12. In the example, student objects are read from a text file, stored in a list, sorted, and sent to output. In a real program that processed student records read from a school's database, you would probably do more than simply sort and show the records, but that just adds more of the same to our example. So to avoid getting lost in the details, we'll just sort and show the records on the console screen.

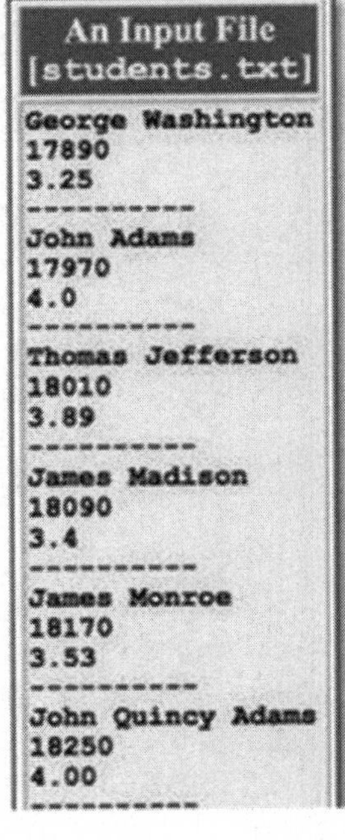

An Input File
[students.txt]

```
George Washington
17890
3.25
----------
John Adams
17970
4.0
----------
Thomas Jefferson
18010
3.89
----------
James Madison
18090
3.4
----------
James Monroe
18170
3.53
----------
John Quincy Adams
18250
4.00
----------
```

```
Andrew Jackson
18290
3.27
----------
Martin Van Buren
18370
3.10
----------
William Harrison
18410
3.67
----------
John Tyler
18411
3.39
----------
James Polk
18450
3.91
----------
Zachary Taylor
18490
3.95
----------
```

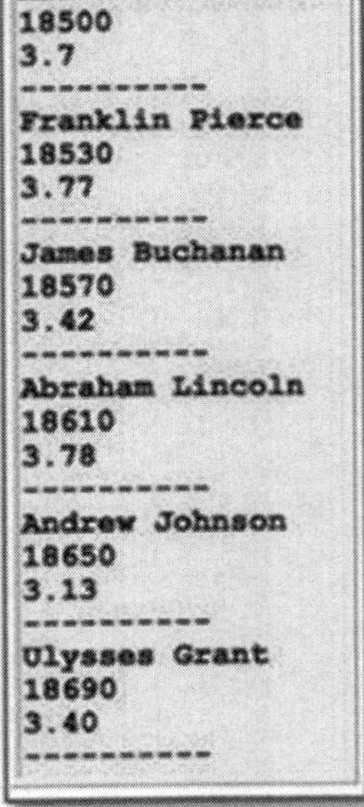

```
Millard Fillmore
18500
3.7
----------
Franklin Pierce
18530
3.77
----------
James Buchanan
18570
3.42
----------
Abraham Lincoln
18610
3.78
----------
Andrew Johnson
18650
3.13
----------
Ulysses Grant
18690
3.40
----------
```

Processing Student Records In A List [studentList.py]

```
class Student:
  name = None
  id = None
  gpa = None
# Student specification ends here

def outputStudents(student, nStudents):
  for i in range(nStudents):
    print("Name =", "{:30}".format(student[i].name), end="")
    print(" ID =", "{:07}".format(student[i].id), end="")
    print(", gpa =", student[i].gpa)
# outputStudents ends here

# main program starts here
try: # open a file for input
  fin = open("students.txt")

  # create an empty list
  MAX_STUDENTS = 30 # list capacity
  nStudents = 0 # initially empty list
  student = [Student() for i in range(MAX_STUDENTS)]
except:
  print("file not found")
  exit() # end the program NOW

# read and save the records
for lineFromFile in fin:
  aStudent = Student()
  aStudent.name = lineFromFile.strip()
  aStudent.id = int(fin.readline().strip())
  aStudent.gpa = float(fin.readline().strip())
  fin.readline() # skip the ---------- separator

  # add record to list, if it's not full
  if (nStudents < MAX_STUDENTS):
    student[nStudents] = aStudent
    nStudents += 1
fin.close() # done with the file

# sort the students by name
for i in range(nStudents):
  for j in range(i + 1, nStudents):
    if student[i].name.lower() > student[j].name.lower():
      student[i],student[j] = student[j],student[i]

outputStudents(student, nStudents)
```

Let's look at what just happened. Note that the input text file has ---------- separating each student's data – this is to make the file easier for humans to read. You see in the main program that there is code to skip the separator.

The lowercase versions of the names are used to sort the objects, low to high alphabetically. If you wanted to make the comparison based on ID or gpa, you would rewrite the comparison statement. Here are alternate sort comparisons for the other fields in `Student`:

```
if student[i].id > student[j].id: # then swap
  student[i],student[j] = student[j],student[i]

if student[i].gpa > student[j].gpa: # then swap
  student[i],student[j] = student[j],student[i]
```

The "outputStudents" function has two values in its parameter list: the array and its associated size counter. In order to print the name in a left-justified column of 30 characters, and to pad the IDs with leading zeros, there's some pretty fancy formatting going on! Instead of printing just `student[i].name`, it's `"{:30}".format(student[i].name)`. The 30 sets the width of the name output to 30 columns, adding spaces at the end of each name that's less than 30 characters so that each name takes exactly 30.

Then, instead of printing just `student[i].id`, it's `"{:07}".format(student[i].id)`. The 7 sets the width of the output to 7 columns, but there's an extra feature – it's not just 7, it's 07. The 0 means to pad from the front with zeros.

With all of the details moved to functions, the main program is pretty easy to follow.

13.4 Exercises, Sample Code, Videos, And Addendums

Go to www.rdb3.com/python/13 for extended materials pertaining to this chapter.

Chapter 14. Lists Of Unlimited Size: Linked Lists

As in the previous chapter, the purpose of this chapter is *not* to train you in the use of linked lists. It is instead an opportunity to introduce concepts that you will run into if you go further in your study of computer science, and to provide an application of the programming features we studied in preceding chapters for the sake of practicing what you've just learned. So try to understand the "link" concept as you study this chapter, knowing that you will explore it in detail in future studies. Focus on the applications of variables, branching, loops, objects, and functions.

There are two problems with array-based lists: (1) they have a limited capacity, and (2) if you do not use them to their capacity, you've wasted memory. "Linked lists" solve the capacity problem. There is no limit specification! A limit was inherent in array-based lists, because a number needed to be used in the declaration of the array. But not so with linked lists! Also, there are no wasted elements in linked lists, because the list only contains values that were specifically linked in.

A drawback of linked lists is that they require that their values be *objects*. If you want a simple list of numbers or text, you have to put a field in an object specification, which may only have that one field. This may seem like a lot of overhead and extra work, but in most applications, linked lists are used with objects anyway, so the object specification already exists in most cases, and all you do is add another field – a "next-link".

14.1 The Next-Link

The values contained in linked lists are objects. In order for an object to be suitable for use in a linked list, its object specification needs to contain a "next-link" to the next object. Mostly, objects do not have links in them – but objects intended for use in linked lists do. The next-link is normally the *last* field in the object specification, and it is usually named "next".

An Object Specification For Use In A Linked List
```
class Student:
  name = None
  id = None
  gpa = None
  next = None # the "next-link"
# Student specification ends here
```

Objects containing a next-link are called "nodes"

14.2 The Start-Link

The identifier for a linked list is its "start-link". Here is how to declare an *empty* linked list:

```
start = None # the start-link declaration
```

While it is not required, and some programmers and textbooks do not do so, linked lists should *always* start out empty. That's what the `None` does in the declaration statement.

By convention, the identifier for a linked list is named `start`. But if you have more than one list in the same scope, they obviously cannot have the same identifier, so other names can, of course, be used.

A value of `None`, which is a Python keyword, indicates that the list is *empty*. A value other than `None` would be the first node in the list.

14.3 Building A Linked List

Nodes can easily be added and removed anywhere in a linked list. But in this book we only show how to add and remove nodes to the *front* of a list, leaving other linked list features for future study.

14.3.1 Adding A Node To A Linked List

There are 3 steps to adding a node. The first is to *create* the node. The second is to *assign values* to the node's data fields – all but its next-link. The last is to *link the new node* into the list.

Here's the code for creating and adding a node:

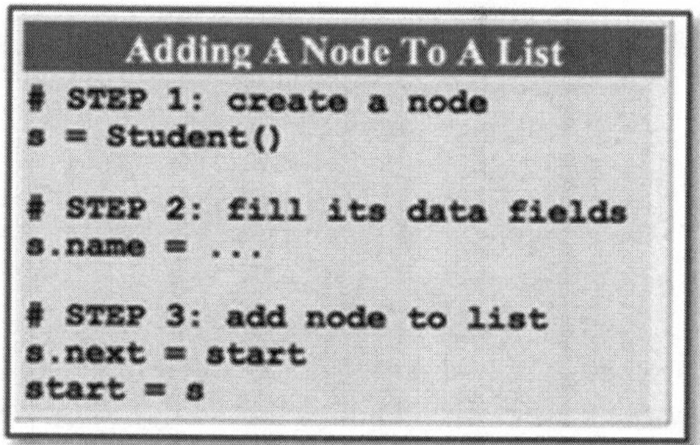

Adding A Node To A List

```
# STEP 1: create a node
s = Student()

# STEP 2: fill its data fields
s.name = ...

# STEP 3: add node to list
s.next = start
start = s
```

14.3.2 Removing A Value From A Linked List

Here's a simple code-block to remove the last-added value from the list, storing its value in a temporary object for processing.

Removing The Last-Added Node

```
aStudent = start # remove node
start = start.next # relink the linked list
```

14.3.3 Start-Links, Next-Links, And Nodes – Oh, My!

Okay, so the code for linked lists can be given to you as it has above, but what does it all really mean? Conceptually, arrays are fairly easy to understand. An array is like a classroom with students' desks all laid out in orderly rows. An array-based list is like filling those desks starting with the left-most one in the front-most row, and working to the right until the first row is filled, and then continuing to the next row. By keeping track of the number of students already in the room (using a list size variable), the instructor can *compute* the location of the desk to assign to the next-arriving student.

By contrast, a linked list is like a room with desks, tables, displays, and other structures scattered about. It starts out with an instructor, but no students, because they have not arrived yet.

When the first student arrives and chooses a desk, and the instructor writes on an index card the *desk's* location in the room – not the student's name or ID, just there the *desk* is. When the second student arrives and chooses desk, the instructor *hands off* the index card to the newly arriving student – it's now the new student's job to track that. The instructor makes a new index card to track where the *new* arrival is, to replace the one given to the new student. This continues as more students arrive.

The instructor can always find all the students in the room because the instructor's index card notes where the last-arriving student is, and that student can direct the instructor to another student because it's written on the index card given to them by the instructor when they arrived. This continues until the first-arriving student is found, who has no index card. In the following diagram, Thomas arrived first, then John, then George.

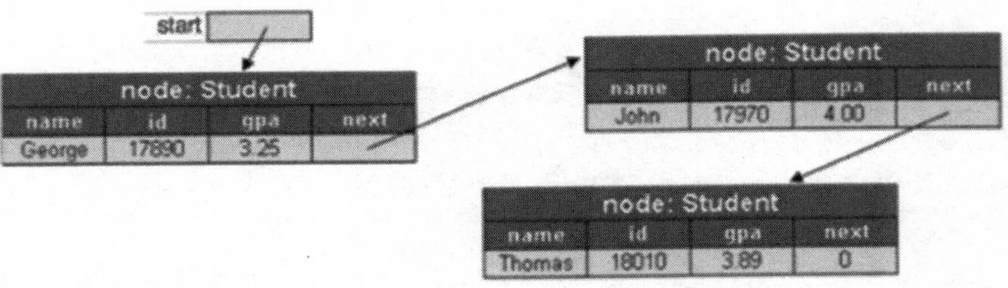

The instructor's index card is the *start-link*, noting where the last-arriving student can be found. Each student is a *node*, because besides having a name, ID, and other student-related data, they also have a *next-link* – the index card with where the student who arrived before them can be found. The *first-arriving* student has no index card.

14.4 Traversing Linked Lists

We use a for-loop to traverse arrays and array-based lists. We also use a for-loop to traverse linked lists. But the loop looks a bit different:

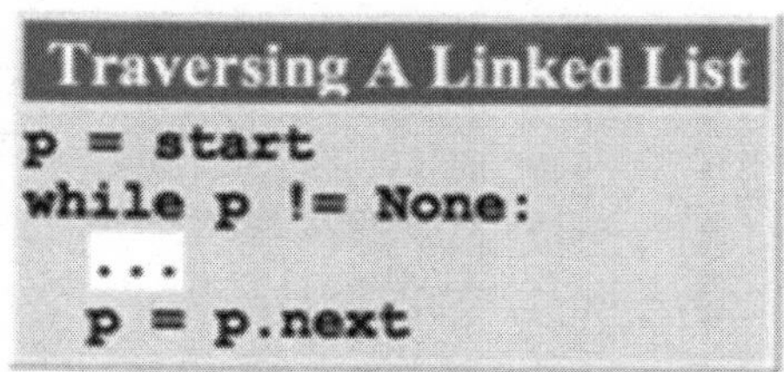

p is like an erasable index card in our classroom example above. It starts out with a copy of what's on the instructor's index card, **p = start**, and the first cycle of the loop uses that value – the location of the last-arriving student. After that cycle, the value on the **p** index card is scratched out and overwritten with what's on the last-arriving student's index card, **p = p.next**, and cycles continue until the cycle for the first-arriving student (without an index card) completes.

Inside the loop's code block, the fields are accessed with these expressions: **p.name**, **p.id**, and **p.gpa**. It looks something like this – note the addition of a box labeled "p":

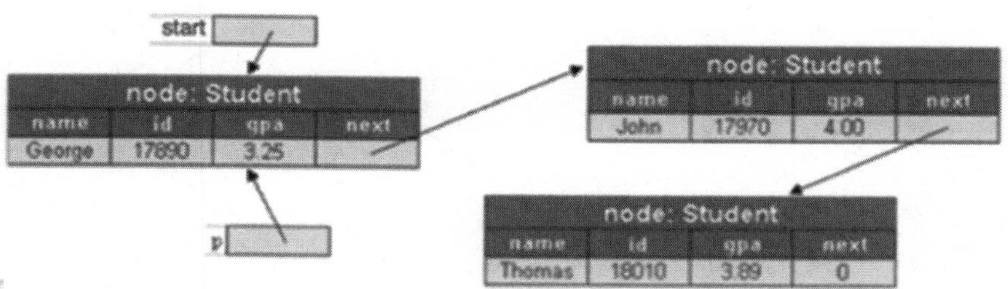

Conceptual representation

p starts out referring to the same node that **start** refers to, as depicted above where it points to George. This is accomplished in the code by the expression `p = start`. Then before the second cycle of the loop, it moves so that it refers to the second node in the list, and so on. The moving of `p` from one node to the next is accomplished in the code by the expression `p = p.next`. This continues until `p` finally reaches the last node and ends up with a value of `None`.

14.4.1 Getting The Size Of A Linked List

Array-based lists use a variable to track their size. But not so with linked lists! While it is certainly possible to have a variable for linked list size, we're not doing so here. Here's how to find the size of a linked list – by traversing and counting:

Counting The Nodes In A Linked List

```
size = 0
p = start
while p != None:
  size += 1
  p = p.next
```

14.5 A Linked List Example

Here is **studentList.py** rewritten using a linked list. There is no sorting. Linked list sorting is a bit complicated, and we leave that for future study. Also, functions are left out for simplicity's sake.

Processing Student Records In A Linked List [studentLinkedList.py]

```
class Student:
  name = None
  id = None
  gpa = None
  next = None # the "next-link"
# Student specification ends here

# main program starts here
try: # open a file for input
  fin = open("students.txt")
  start = None # create an empty list
except:
  print("file not found")
  exit() # end the program NOW

# read and save the records
for lineFromFile in fin:
  aStudent = Student() # Step 1, create a node

  # Step 2, read its data fields
  aStudent.name = lineFromFile.strip()
  aStudent.id = int(fin.readline().strip())
  aStudent.gpa = float(fin.readline().strip())
  fin.readline() # skip the ---------- separator

  # Step 3, add new node to the list
  aStudent.next = start
  start = aStudent
fin.close() # done with the input file

# traverse the list and output
p = start
while p != None:
  print("Name = {:30}".format(p.name), end="")
  print(" ID = {:07}".format(p.id), end="")
  print(", gpa =", p.gpa)
  p = p.next
```

14.6 A Linked Lists Of Whole Numbers

As previously explained, you cannot have a linked list of numbers or text values without first enclosing them in an object. So here is an example that reads whole numbers from the keyboard, stores them in a linked list, and sends their average to the console display:

Putting Whole Numbers Into A Linked List [intLinkedList.py]

```
class Score:
  value = None
  next = None # the "next-link"
# Score specification ends here

# main program starts here
start = None # create an empty list

# read and save the records
while True:
  aScore = Score() # Step 1, create a node

  # Step 2, read its data fields
  aScore.value = int(input("Enter a score [-1 to quit]: "))
  if (aScore.value == -1): break

  # Step 3, add new node to the list
  aScore.next = start
  start = aScore

# traverse the list and get the average
count = 0
total = 0
p = start
while p != None:
  total += p.value
  count += 1
  p = p.next

# output the result
if count > 0:
  average = total / count
  print("The average of", count, "scores is", average)
else:
  print("No values were entered.")
```

14.7 Exercises, Sample Code, Videos, And Addendums

Go to www.rdb3.com/python/14 for extended materials pertaining to this chapter.

Chapter 15. Some Advanced Topics

This book is an introduction to the world of computer programming. Its purpose was to turn you into a computer programmer, and if you got this far, it probably succeeded. On the later topics starting with lists (array-based and linked) only some beginning concepts were developed. For example, we did not show how to add and remove values anywhere except the end of array-based lists, and did not even mention the possibility of expanding list capacity. For linked lists we showed how to add and remove nodes at the front of a list, but did not show how to do so anywhere else, and did not deal with sorting or function calls. All of these are topics for further study in computer programming, and perhaps your study so far has inspired you to go on from here.

Before we complete our introduction, though, we want to expose you to a couple of additional programming topics: collections and recursion. They are unrelated to each other, except for the fact that they are more advanced topics in computer science. Collections, because you should not have to write array-based and linked list code the rest of your programming life. Recursion, because it is a subject that you will have to hear about more than once before you believe that it works, so we may as well start now!

15.1 The Easy Way: Collections

In modern computer languages, the details of array-based and linked list code has already been optimized by professional programmers and put into modules for you to use. The "list" in Python manages the details, without the programmer having to worry about capacity or start-links and next-links. To declare an empty list of Student objects, use the following:

This can be used for whole number and floating point data types as well as objects, because there is no reference to `Student` or to anything that would indicate the type of data to be stored in the list!

To add a value to the front or end of a list, use the following:

Adding A Value To A Collection

```
for... # or while
  aStudent = Student() # a temporary object

  # set field values for aStudent
  aStudent.name = ...

  student[:0] = [aStudent] # copy to the front

  ... or ...

  student[len(student):] = [aStudent] # copy to the end
```

To retrieve a value from *any* position in the collection, use the following expression:

```
student[i]
```

`i` is an *index*, as in an array, and can be any number in the range `0` to `len(student) - 1`, inclusive. To get the value at the front, it's `student[0]`, and at the end, it's `student[len(student) - 1]`. And just like array objects, collections "know" their own size – `len(student]`. The difference is that we did not change array sizes after they got created – collection sizes *do* change with every addition.

Also, as with array elements, the expression `student[i]` can be used on either side of an assignment operator (that is, an equal sign), to retrieve or set the value in the collection.

This is not demonstrated in any code examples in this chapter, but it is included in the discussion here for completeness. Here is our code example from the previous chapter, but adapted for using collections:

Processing Student Records In A Collection [studentCollection.py]

```
class Student:
  name = None
  id = None
  gpa = None
# Student specification ends here

def outputStudents(student):
  for i in range(len(student)):
    print("Name = {:30}".format(student[i].name), end="")
    print(" ID = {:07}".format(student[i].id), end="")
    print(", gpa =", student[i].gpa)
# outputStudents ends here

# main program starts here
try: # open a file for input
  fin = open("students.txt")
  student = [] # an empty collection
except:
  print("file not found")
  exit() # end the program NOW

# read and save the records
for lineFromFile in fin:
  aStudent = Student()
  aStudent.name = lineFromFile.strip()
  aStudent.id = int(fin.readline().strip())
  aStudent.gpa = float(fin.readline().strip())
  fin.readline() # skip the ---------- separator

  student[len(student):] = [aStudent] # copy to the end
fin.close() # done with the file

outputStudents(student)
```

Note that the function parameter list includes a specification for the collection.

15.2 Functions That Call Themselves: Recursion

Recursion is simply this – it's when the code block of a function contains a statement with a call to itself! This actually is a form of a loop, which would seem to be infinite. What makes it work is that the function must contain logic to decide whether to continue calling itself or not – similar to if-break in a while-true loop.

Recursion offers a new way to solve problems. If you are not using recursion, you are using "iteration" – it's what we have been using all along, but since it was the only thing we used, it really did not need a name. Iteration uses loops; recursion uses functions.

Recursion is usually an upper-level computer science topic. It is very useful in solving some types of problems, and actually *simplifies* many solutions. So if it's so simple, why is it at the end of this book, and why is it upper-level? That's because it is difficult for most people to understand right away – even people with strong aptitudes for computers. This is something that you will have to hear now and believe later!

To apply recursion, you just need to know these things about the problem you are solving: (1) how to solve a base case, and (2) how to reduce problem complexity towards a base case. Then you need to be able to divide problems into two parts: (1) the part you know how to solve, and (2) the part you don't know how to solve.

15.2.1 Simple Example: Countdown

This ridiculously easy example demonstrates the sequence for developing a recursive solution. The problem is this: NASA has hired you to write a countdown program, starting from any non-negative whole number and ending at zero. (NASA uses this kind of thing a lot, and they want to automate it!) You first consider using an *iterative* solution, but you soon conclude that it is just too difficult (work with me here...). So you next consider using a *recursive* solution instead.

The problem, then, is this: count down from the positive, whole number stored in the variable `n`. First, write down the part you know how to do: say the number stored in `n`. Then write down the part you don't know how to do: count down from `n` minus one. For example, if `n` is "10", the recursive solution is to say "10", and then count down from "9". If you wrote a function to do this, and the number to count down from is in the parameter list, the body of the function would do these two things: output the variable from the parameter list, and then call a function that knows how to count down from that value minus one. And here's the tricky part – the function we would call to do that is the function we are currently writing! Seems a bit like the chicken-and-the-egg dilemma, doesn't it.

The only problem that remains is to identify a "base case", and use that in a logic statement to stop the recursion. The base case is this: if we were asked to count down from zero, it would be easy – just say "0"! In that case, if the value of the variable in the parameter list is zero, no additional call needs to be made.

Here is the full solution (which you are free to copy, modify, and share with NASA – you're welcome):

Recursive Countdown [countDown.py]

```
def countDown(n):
  print(n, end = " ") # the part I know how to do
  if n > 0: # look for base case
    countDown(n - 1) # do this if not base case
# countDown ends here

# main program starts here
n = int(input("Enter n: "))
countDown(n)
print()
```

15.2.2 Classic Example: Factorial

The classic introductory example for recursion is factorial. In math class you may have seen a symbol like this: **5!**, pronounced "five factorial". It is the equivalent of 5 x 4 x 3 x 2 x 1, or 120. Factorials show up in probability calculations for such things as lotteries.

The problem is this: we want a function to calculate the factorial of a non-negative number, **n**. First we consider coming up with an iterative solution, and we quickly decide that it is too complicated (again, work with me here). So we consider using recursion. First, there is a base case: **0!** is defined as 1 – actually, **1!** is also 1 – both are base cases. Working towards the base case, **n!** is **n** (the part we know how to solve) times **(n-1)!** (the part we do not know how to solve). Luckily we have a function to solve the latter – the function we are writing! So the recursive solution is **n! = n x (n-1)!**:

The Classic Recursive Factorial [factorial.py]

```
def factorial(n):
  result = 0
  if n < 2: # detecting a base case
    result = 1
  else:
    result = n * factorial(n - 1) # do this if not base case
  return result
# factorial ends here

# main program starts here
n = int(input("Enter n: "))
print(factorial(n))
```

15.2.3 A Caution...

Do not get too attached to recursion. There is always an iterative solution to everything – it's just that recursion is sometimes simpler to code, once you get familiar enough with it. But recursion is usually less efficient than iteration, so use iteration if you can. Use recursion as a convenience, realizing that there is a cost involved. And sometimes that cost is too much, even for the easiest of recursive solutions – try counting down from 100000 and see! If that works, then try a million...

15.3 Where Do We Go From Here?

This introduction to programming used Python to make the concepts real. These concepts, such as variables, code blocks, branching and looping logic, subprograms, arrays, and lists, are common to all programming languages. What you learned here actually serves as the introduction that you would need to go on to the study of *any* specific language – not just Python.

If this is where you end your study of programming, then hopefully you found this interesting and enlightening, and you have a better understanding of how computers work and what computer programming professionals do. If this is just the beginning for you, then you are ready to master one or more languages and then learn techniques of problem solving. You will likely eventually learn to develop user interfaces and write GUI (graphical user interface) programs. You may learn to be a solo programmer or a member of a team of programmers. You may write scientific simulations, business databases, or interactive games. Whatever you do, it's a great profession with an unlimited future, and you will always be glad you found your way into it!

Appendix: Standard Python Functions

Here is a compilation of all the functions from the Python modules, which are used in this book. The table below lists models of expressions and the module that needs to be imported in order to use the expression, if any.

identifier	import module
fabs(*number*)	*none*
float(*expression*)	*none*
input(*prompt*)	*none*
int(*expression*)	*none*
len(*array or variable with text*)	*none*
open(*filename*)	*none*
math.pow(*number, number*)	**math**
print(*expression(s)*)	*none*
random.randint(*number, number*)	**random**
time.sleep(*number*)	**time**
math.sqrt(*number*)	**math**

Index

H

I

J

L

M

N

O

P